Patti B. Geil, MS, RD, FADA, CDE, and Tami A. Ross, RD, CDE

Diabetes
Meals
on $7 a Day
or Less

⚠ ®American Diabetes Association

Book Acquisitions	Robert J. Anthony
Editor	Aime M. Ballard
Production Director	Carolyn R. Segree
Production Coordinator	Peggy M. Rote
Composition	Harlowe Typography, Inc.
Text and Cover Design	Wickham & Associates, Inc.

Printed in Canada

1 3 5 7 9 10 8 6 4 2

The suggestions and information contained in this publication are generally consistent with the *Clinical Practice Recommendations* and other policies of the American Diabetes Association, but they do not represent the policy or position of the Association or any of its boards or committees. Reasonable steps have been taken to ensure the accuracy of the information presented. However, the American Diabetes Association cannot ensure the safety or efficacy of any product or service described in this publication. Individuals are advised to consult a physician or other appropriate health care professional before undertaking any diet or exercise program or taking any medication referred to in this publication. Professionals must use and apply their own professional judgment, experience, and training and should not rely solely on the information contained in this publication before prescribing any diet, exercise, or medication. The American Diabetes Association—its officers, directors, employees, volunteers, and members—assumes no responsibility or liability for personal or other injury, loss, or damage that may result from the suggestions or information in this publication.

ADA titles may be purchased for business or promotional use or for special sales. For information, please write to: Lee M. Romano, Special Sales & Promotions, at the address below.

American Diabetes Association
1660 Duke Street
Alexandria, Virginia 22314

Library of Congress Cataloging-in-Publication Data

Geil, Patti Bazel.
    Diabetes meals on $7 a day—or less: how to plan healthy menus without breaking the bank / by Patti B. Geil and Tami A. Ross.
       p. cm.
    Includes index.
    ISBN 1-58040-023-X (pbk.)
    1. Diabetes—Diet therapy—Recipes.   2. Low budget cookery.
I. Ross, Tami. II. Title.
RC662.G45 1999
641.5'6314—dc21

98–54451
CIP

Contents

Healthy Eating: A Blue-Chip Investment

I t is just a quick trip to the supermarket "to pick up a few things." You reach the end of the checkout line and you're suddenly slammed with "sticker shock." How could just a few bags of groceries cost more than a hundred dollars? You know that healthy eating is vitally important for people with diabetes, yet once again you find yourself thinking, "I can't afford to eat healthfully!"

Without a doubt, diabetes is an expensive disease. It costs Americans $98.2 billion in direct medical costs every year. On an individual basis, family budgets must stretch to cover the costs of medications, monitoring supplies, and more frequent visits to health care providers. Many people also have the notion that a healthy diabetes diet must be costly. They think that it requires special "dietetic" or "diabetic" foods and high-priced sugar-free treats. The average American household already spends 12 cents of every dollar of its disposable income on food. Given the additional expenses associated with proper medical management of diabetes, economics may pose a serious roadblock to following an ideal meal plan. Recognizing this roadblock, reviewing your cash register tapes, and revising your meal planning and shopping strategies will save you money without shortchanging your health.

Investing a bit of time and money in healthy eating is a blue-chip investment in your future. The results of the Diabetes Control and Complications Trial (DCCT) show that improving blood glucose control lowers the risk of diabetes complications, such as eye and kidney disease. Nutrition is a key factor in helping to control your diabetes. Spending the money to eat healthfully will improve blood glucose control now and help prevent costly complications and expensive medical care later.

Eating well and spending less are not mutually exclusive. If you think you must buy high-priced "special" versions of the foods your family usually eats, think again! Sugar-free soft drinks and fat-free foods can certainly enhance your diet if your budget allows, but the American Diabetes Association nutrition recommendations suggest that you should simply eat healthfully—the same advice that applies to every member of your family. The nutrition guidance for people with diabetes is the same as that for anyone interested in eating for good health: a plate full of low-fat, high-fiber grains, beans, fruits, and vegetables with small portions of meats and protein foods and limited amounts of fats, sweets, and alcohol. Everyone in the house should strive to eat according to these guidelines to lower the risk of heart disease, obesity, and some forms of cancer. Involve your family in your healthy-eating, cost-cutting campaign. They—and your wallet—will thank you.

So leave those costly so-called diet or diabetic foods on the shelf. Hands off the high-priced sugar-free sweets. The latest nutrition recommendations give you the freedom to enjoy small amounts of regular sugar and sweets, as long as your weight, blood glucose levels, and blood lipids (blood fats) remain in control. If you used to spend significant amounts of money on artificially sweetened treats, now you can use your savings to invest in another good-for-you treat, such as a new exercise video or a stress-free evening on the town.

Spend Less, Eat Healthy

Everyone loves to save money, no matter what his or her bank account balance. This book will guide you in your quest to eat healthfully on a lean budget. As you will see, economical diabetes meal planning doesn't mean deboning countless chickens, serving endless meals of leftovers, or driving all over town for grocery store specials. You may be surprised to find you can even take an occasional night off kitchen duty for a carefully chosen fast-food meal.

The recipes in this book are simple and quick to assemble, with an emphasis on easy-to-find ingredients. If you are eligible for food assistance programs, such as food stamps, WIC (Women, Infants and Children), or Meals-on-Wheels, you'll find that the recipes and menus in this book will help you make the most of the foods available through these sources. Pick a few new recipes, take a look at the meal plans, and review the shopping tips before your next supermarket safari. You will be pleasantly surprised to find that the small changes we suggest will quickly add up to make you healthier and wealthier. Saving just $5 a week on food fattens your piggy bank by more than $250 a year. You can spend less and eat healthy!

CHAPTER 1

Diabetes Nutrition Guidelines: Healthy, Wealthy, and Wise

D o you think the right foods for your diabetes are too costly for your family's food budget? Maybe you mistakenly believe some of these common diabetes money myths:

- ■ "I can't afford to follow a diabetes diet. It's too expensive."

- ■ "I'll have to spend too much on special foods that the rest of my family won't eat."

- ■ "I can't pay for all the fresh fruits and vegetables and high-priced cuts of meat a diabetes diet requires."

This book was created to dispel these myths and prove that good food does not have to break your budget. The bottom line is that eating foods that are healthy for diabetes shouldn't cost you any more than you're already spending in time, effort, or dollars. A quick review of the current diabetes nutrition guidelines proves that the foods you need for your diabetes are exactly the same foods your entire family needs to promote good health.

Good Food for the Entire Family

If you are concerned that your special diabetes nutrition needs will break the family's food budget, worry no more. The latest diabetes nutrition recommendations parallel the dietary guidelines for all Americans:

- Eat a variety of foods.

- Balance the food you eat with physical activity—maintain or improve your weight.

- Eat plenty of grain products, vegetables, and fruits.

- Choose foods that are low in total fat, saturated fat, and cholesterol.

- Eat only moderate amounts of sugars.

- Eat a moderate amount of salt and sodium.

- If you drink alcoholic beverages, do so in moderation.

Diabetes Food Goals for You

The first diabetes diet recommendations were made in Egypt in 1550 B.C. and consisted of wheat grains, fresh grits, grapes, honey, and sweet beer. Times have changed! The American Diabetes Association nutrition recommendations stress an overall healthy eating plan. Several nutrients deserve special attention. Meet with your registered dietitian to discuss:

- *Calories:* The days of preprinted, calorie-level diet sheets are over. Although we know that most adults require between 1,800 and 2,500 calories per day, what you need to maintain a reasonable body weight may be different. Individualized meal plans, designed with the help of a registered dietitian, are the best.

- *Protein:* Your intake of protein foods (meats, poultry, seafood, and dairy foods) should be at the same level as that of the general public. These foods should make up between 10 and 20% of the calories you eat. This translates into two

3-ounce servings (3 ounces is about the size of a deck of cards or the palm of a woman's hand) each day. There is some evidence that vegetable protein, which comes from foods such as beans, grains, and vegetables, may slow the rate of kidney disease in people with diabetes. Eating less protein from animal sources, such as meat, milk, eggs, and cheese, also means less fat, saturated fat, and cholesterol in your diet.

■ *Fat:* A lower fat intake lowers your risk for cardiovascular (heart) disease, a common complication of diabetes. Lower fat intake means lower calorie intake, which also helps you maintain a reasonable body weight. Limit animal protein and whole-milk dairy foods to eat less fat and cholesterol. Your cholesterol intake should be less than 300 milligrams per day. The exact amount and type of fat you should eat will depend on your weight, your blood lipid levels, and your overall health.

■ *Carbohydrate:* There is no scientific evidence that sugar raises your blood glucose any faster than carbohydrates from starchy foods such as pasta, potatoes, bread, and cereal. But this does not mean your diet should be planned around candy, sweet rolls, and soft drinks! High-sugar foods are often high in calories and fat, but low in nutrients. Your sugar intake should be moderate, just as the guidelines for the general public state. For people with diabetes, the total amount of carbohydrate eaten in a day, rather than the type, has the most direct effect on blood glucose. There is no need for you to spend money on special "diabetic" foods unless you enjoy their taste or the variety they provide. Sweeteners such as corn syrup, fruit juice, and sorbitol may offer no advantage over regular table sugar. Enjoy sweet treats in moderation. Substitute them for other carbohydrates in your diet, and check your blood glucose to see how they affect you.

■ *Fiber:* You should be eating the same amount of fiber as the other members of your family: 20–35 grams/day. Unfortunately, most Americans eat only 10–13 grams daily, so they don't reap fiber's benefits, such as better digestive health. Choose whole-wheat grains and plenty of fresh fruits and vegetables every day. Oats and dried beans are great sources of soluble fiber, which has a positive effect on your blood lipid levels.

■ *Sodium:* Sodium intake recommendations for people with diabetes are the same as those for the general population: less than 3,000 milligrams per day. If you have high blood pressure, you may want to limit your sodium to 2,400 milligrams per day. Shake the salt habit, and carefully read food labels to track the amount of sodium in your diet.

■ *Alcohol:* Don't consume more than one or two alcoholic beverages daily (one drink equals 12 ounces of beer, 5 ounces of wine, or 1 1/2 ounces of distilled alcohol [liquor]). After having an alcoholic drink, check your blood glucose to see its effect. The calories in alcohol are empty of nutrients. Alcohol can raise certain blood fats and may cause low blood glucose. Do you really want to break your budget for beer? Use caution!

■ *Vitamins and minerals:* You may be a candidate for vitamin and mineral supplements if you are in poor diabetes control; if you are on a very restricted weight-loss diet; if you are elderly, pregnant, or breast-feeding; or if you are a strict vegetarian. Eating a well-balanced diet should provide everyone with the essential vitamins and minerals they require. However, you should ask your health care team to discuss your specialized vitamin and mineral needs.

Smart Choices

The recent revolution in diabetes nutrition may have left you more confused than ever. A session with a registered dietitian and certified diabetes educator (RD, CDE) is money and time well invested. A registered dietitian can evaluate your individual case and suggest the meal planning approach that is best for you, whether it is the Diabetes Food Pyramid or carbohydrate counting or something in between.

■ To find a registered dietitian near you, call The American Dietetic Association's National Center for Nutrition and

Dietetics at 1-800-366-1655. Ask for a specialist in diabetes nutrition.

■ To find a diabetes educator in your area, call the American Association of Diabetes Educators at 1-800-832-6874.

■ To find a diabetes education program in your area, call 1-800-DIABETES or log onto the American Diabetes Association's website at www.diabetes.org.

Making smart food choices is the key to taking care of your diabetes. Poor choices will cost you time, money, and your health. Eating well helps keep your blood glucose in control. It helps you avoid the expensive damage to your eyes, heart, and kidneys that occurs when blood glucose levels are high day after day. You can eat healthfully on a lean budget by using the diabetes nutrition guidelines to make smart food choices. Keep this example in mind: Five pounds of naturally fat-free baking potatoes costs $1.99. In contrast, you'll pay $17.08 for 5 pounds of high-fat potato chips. It's easy to see which choice is better for your budget—and your health!

CHAPTER 2

Economy Gastronomy: Penny-Wise Meal Planning, Cost-Wise Cooking

Penny-wise meal planning and cost-wise cooking are the first steps to stretching your food dollar while eating healthfully. The U.S. Department of Agriculture (USDA) has estimated that a family of four can eat at home for a cost of $95.40 to $184.50 a week. That's only $3.40 to $6.59 per person per day—the cost of just one fast-food value meal. Sound impossible? It's not. Eating healthfully on a lean budget does require a small investment of your time to plan your meals for the week and to cook the foods that match your budget and diabetes nutrition requirements. But the time you spend is an investment that really pays off!

Penny-Wise Meal Planning

Like most Americans, you are probably pressed for time. You often eat meals on the run. Why should you use even a few of your precious moments for meal planning? Take a closer look at the long-term savings in money, time, and health that come with taking the time to think ahead about what you'll be eating. Planning your meals a week in advance enables you to:

- *Take advantage of special sales.* Review your newspaper's grocery store advertisements and find the foods that fit your budget. Plan your meals around the specials for the week to take a big bite out of your food expenses. Make a list to take to the grocery store.

- *Resist impulse buying.* If you know what you need for the week and stick to your list, you are more likely to avoid high-price/low-nutrition items like snack chips and sugar-free candy.

- *Save time and money.* By planning meals in advance you'll be able to do all of your shopping at one time. You won't have to make several trips to the store to buy foods you forgot. You'll save time and gasoline in addition to money. If you have your menu planned ahead, you'll be able to buy the right kind of food in the package size to fit your needs.

No time to plan? Begin by reviewing the week's menu for a 1,800-calorie meal plan at the end of this chapter. These low-cost meals are planned around recipes found in this book. Use the menu as a starting point to plan your week and make your grocery list. If you are still overwhelmed by the thought of planning a week's worth of menus, start by planning five evening meals, rather than meals for a whole week. You'll find that between using "planned-overs," eating out, and dining at a friend's home, those five meals will stretch into a week's worth of healthful and inexpensive eating. Planning five meals will take only 5 minutes—time you can surely find while waiting for a doctor's appointment or for a pot of pasta to boil.

How do you plan menus? If you are following a diabetes meal planing approach, such as the exchange system, the Diabetes Food Pyramid, or carbohydrate counting, you are already off to a great start. Your meal pattern will tell you which foods you need and how much of each to include. For example, if you are following an exchange diet, you will know how many servings you need from the starch list, vegetable list, fruit list, meat or meat-substitute list, milk list, and fat list each day. If you are following the Diabetes Food Pyramid, use the guidelines on number of servings from each section of the pyramid. The carbohydrate counting system outlines the number of grams of carbohydrate you can use at each meal and snack each day. You choose the food groups and number of servings to meet your target goal. No matter what your method of diabetes meal planning, the foods you eat and the timing of your meals should be based on your personal diabetes medication and on your blood glucose checking results.

Your meal plan, or meal pattern, is the basis of your menu and shopping list for the week. A registered dietitian can help you develop a meal pattern that is right for you. Having your meal pattern gives you the freedom to decide which foods within that pattern meet your budget needs for the week. Need a fruit for lunch? If it's fall, apples are an economical choice. What about a vegetable or salad for dinner? Nothing can beat the great taste—and price—of fresh tomatoes in the summer. To save even more time, keep a master list of all the meals that meet your meal pattern needs. You can select from these tried-and-true combinations rather than plan entirely new menus every week. You will soon accumulate a large list of economical meals. And you can vary your choices to avoid mealtime boredom.

Meatless Days

When you're planning your meals for the week, think about including at least one "meatless day." Smaller amounts of meat in your meal plan mean lower food costs, as well as less saturated fat and cholesterol. You can design meals that provide protein from meat substitutes, such as red beans and rice or vegetable lasagna. And remember, ethnic menus add variety and savings. For example, Chinese meals are often planned around a small amount of inexpensive meat used to flavor other low-cost foods such as rice and cabbage.

Planned-Overs

Leftovers may be your budget's best friend, but no one wants to see the same dish three times in one week. You can save time and money while avoiding mealtime boredom by using "planned-overs," foods intentionally left after a meal to use in another meal. Using planned-overs is quite different from reheating yesterday's supper for today's lunch. When you use planned-overs, you are planning ahead for leftovers. Many of the recipes in this book are designed around the planned-over concept. For example, the chicken left from "Marilyn's Spicy Fried Chicken" (p. 132) is ready for use in "Southwestern Chicken Wrap-Ups" (p. 133). You can plan to use the extra turkey from "Golden Roasted Turkey Breast" (p. 142) in "Tempting Turkey Pot Pie" (p. 140).

If you start thinking about your meals in terms of planned-overs, you'll find easy and interesting examples everywhere. Make a pork roast with vegetables on Sunday, and plan to use the leftover pork later in the week to flavor black beans and rice. Five green peppers can be used in three meals: half of one in a frittata, the other half in pasta primavera, and the rest stuffed with leftover rice or corn for a tasty entrée. A large round steak in a family pack can provide at least four meals. Cut the steak in half lengthwise, then slice one portion into thin strips (across the grain for tenderness) for use in stir-fry and burritos. Freeze the remaining half. You can defrost it at a later date and cube it to make hearty beef stew. If you have scraps left, dice them to use in vegetable beef soup. Be sure to label and date your planned-over foods so that you'll know what you have on hand and use it safely.

Meal Planning Checklist

After you try your hand at planning a week's menu, take a moment to review the checklist below. Do the menus

■ follow your individualized diabetes meal plan?

■ use a variety of foods from all parts of the pyramid?

■ emphasize nutritious, economical foods?

■ take advantage of weekly store specials?

■ include planned-overs?

Cost-Wise Cooking

I said to my wife, 'Where do you want to go for our anniversary?'
She said, 'I want to go somewhere I've never been before.' I said, 'Try
the kitchen.'—Henny Youngman

Cooking is becoming a lost art. But it is one that you'll need
to rediscover if spending less and eating healthfully is your
goal. Fast foods and convenience foods do save time, but they
are real budget-busters. Don't assume that saving money
requires you to become a master chef, slaving for hours over a
hot stove. Start by looking for recipes like those in this book:
quick to assemble, with few ingredients and simple cooking
techniques.

Stock Up

Keep your pantry stocked with low-cost, healthful grocery staples to save time and trips to the store. With basic foods from
these parts of the food pyramid, you'll be ready to cook cost-
wise meals in minutes.

- **Grains, beans, and starchy vegetables:** flour; oats; whole-
  grain breads, cereals, and crackers; dry or canned beans; rice;
  pasta; canned corn; potatoes.

- **Vegetables:** fresh and plain frozen vegetables, tomato sauce,
  canned tomatoes.

- **Fruits:** fresh and plain frozen fruits, fruit canned in juice,
  applesauce, frozen concentrated 100% fruit juice.

- **Milk:** fat-free milk, nonfat dry milk, nonfat yogurt.

- **Meat and others:** chicken, fish, turkey, ground beef, eggs,
  peanut butter, cheese, water-packed canned tuna.

You should also have the right kitchen tools on hand to make
cooking easier. Important pieces for healthful cooking include
a pressure cooker, good-quality sharp knives, a grill, and nonstick cookware. Less expensive tools that should be in your
kitchen are a cheese grater, kitchen shears, a steamer basket, a

kitchen scale, and a cutting board. A microwave is great for reheating your previous night's planned-overs, but you can get more savings from your microwave by using it to

■ Crisp up stale or soggy crackers, cereals, and pretzels. Microwave them in a baking dish on high power until they're very warm (1–3 minutes), stirring once. Let them cool thoroughly to crisp.

■ Get more juice from lemons, oranges, and grapefruits. Slice the fruit in half, then microwave it on high power for 30 seconds to 1 minute.

■ Extract the last drops from a bottle of sugar-free pancake syrup. Remove the cap, then microwave the bottle on high power for 20–30 seconds. An empty-looking bottle may hold as much as 1/4 cup of syrup!

Now You're Cooking!

Once you're in the kitchen, make the most of your time and money by cooking and baking in large quantities and freezing a portion for future meals and snacks. This technique—one way to get planned-overs—is known as batch cooking, and it can be as simple as cooking a few extra chicken breasts to freeze for later use. The idea is to cook once and serve the food two or three times. For example, if you are making pasta for a hot dish at your evening meal, throw some extra noodles in the pot to use in a cold pasta salad for tomorrow's midday meal. Or prepare a large quantity of a standard recipe such as "Spunky Spaghetti Sauce" (p. 143) to use immediately, then freeze the remainder for use in lasagna or stuffed peppers. Make a large batch of waffles on Sunday morning, serve a few for breakfast, and freeze the rest to pop in the toaster on a busy weekday morning.

You may not have time to cook during the workweek, but you may have some free moments on the weekend to prepare food for the week ahead. This saves you not only time, but also money because you buy larger amounts of basic ingredients more economically. Make your own healthful microwave meals by separating your planned-overs into microwave-safe dishes in portion sizes that are right for your individual meal plan. For extra savings, recycle the plates from commercial frozen dinners to use for your meals. Knowing you have something in your freezer that is just a few microwave minutes away from a meal may be just the incentive you need to skip the expensive fast-food drive-through after work.

Clever, cost-wise cooks know the value of casseroles. These one-dish meals can be prepared ahead and stored in the refrigerator or freezer, ready to bake at a moment's notice. Casseroles are a great place to use leftover—or planned-over— turkey, chicken, beef, rice, and vegetables. This makes for less expensive meals and faster baking. Casseroles can be designed to provide you with foods from each of the food groups in your diabetes meal plan. Take a look at the inexpensive, mix-and-match ingredients in the "Quick Six" casserole plan (pp. 14–16) and invent your own one-dish meal. If you plan to cook your prepared casserole within 24 hours or so, store it raw in the refrigerator and allow about 10–15 minutes of extra oven time to make sure the chilled ingredients are baked through. If you decide to freeze the casserole for future use, wrap the dish securely and freeze it for up to 6 weeks. Defrost it thoroughly and safely before baking.

Safety First

Economical eating requires special attention to food safety, particularly when using planned-overs and storing large amounts of foods. For the person with diabetes, the nausea, vomiting, diarrhea, and inability to eat that accompany food-borne illness not only are unpleasant, but also may have serious effects on blood glucose control. For safety first in the cost-wise kitchen, pay attention to "sell by" and "use by" dates on the canned, jarred, and packaged foods you purchase. Safe food storage is essential. Store flour and grains in airtight containers and your canned goods in a cool area. Your refrigerator should be set at 40°F or below, while your freezer should be 0°F or colder. When putting away your groceries, keep these additional safety tips in mind:

Looking for a quick and easy way to plan an inexpensive, yet healthful meal? Use the "Quick Six" casserole plan, a way to mix and match basic ingredients to add variety to economical eating. Ideas range from a classic chicken casserole built around chicken soup, broccoli, rice, chicken, parmesan cheese, and breadcrumbs to a vegetarian casserole made from diced tomatoes, yellow squash, olives, celery, bell pepper, garlic, Parmesan cheese, and bread crumbs.

1. Choose one sauce-maker

- 1 can (10 3/4 oz) reduced-fat cream of mushroom soup, undiluted
- 1 can (10 3/4 oz) reduced-fat cream of celery soup, undiluted
- 1 can (10 3/4 oz) reduced-fat cream of chicken soup, undiluted
- 1 can (10 3/4 oz) cheddar cheese soup, undiluted
- 1 can (10 3/4 oz) cream of potato soup, undiluted
- 2 cans (14 1/2 oz) Italian-style diced tomatoes, drained

2. Choose one frozen vegetable

- 1 package (10 oz) frozen chopped spinach, thawed
- 1 package (10 oz) frozen cut broccoli, thawed
- 1 package (10 oz) frozen French-style green beans, thawed
- 1 package (10 oz) frozen peas, thawed
- 1 package (16 oz) frozen sliced yellow squash, thawed

■ 1 package (10 oz) frozen whole kernel corn, thawed

■ 1 package (10 oz) frozen mixed vegetables, thawed

3. Choose one pasta/rice/potato

■ 2 cups cooked elbow macaroni

■ 1 cup uncooked rice

■ 4 cups uncooked cholesterol-free wide egg noodles

■ 3 cups uncooked medium pasta shells

■ 3 cups frozen shredded hash brown potatoes, thawed

4. Choose one meat/fish/poultry

■ 2 cans (6 oz each) water-packed solid white tuna, drained and flaked

■ 2 cups chopped cooked chicken

■ 2 cups chopped cooked ham

■ 2 cups chopped cooked turkey

■ 1 lb lean ground turkey or beef, browned and drained

5. Choose one or more extras (optional)

■ 1 can (3 oz) sliced mushrooms, drained

■ 1/2 cup sliced ripe olives

■ 1/4 cup chopped bell pepper

■ 1/4 cup chopped onion

■ 1/2 cup chopped celery

■ 1/4 cup shredded carrot

continued on next page

continued from previous page

- 2 garlic cloves, minced
- 1 can (4 1/2 oz) chopped green chili peppers
- 1 package (1 1/4 oz) taco seasoning mix

6. Choose one or two toppings

- 1/2 cup (2 oz) shredded low-fat mozzarella cheese
- 1/2 cup grated Parmesan cheese
- 1/2 cup (2 oz) shredded low-fat Swiss cheese
- 1/2 cup (2 oz) shredded low-fat cheddar cheese
- 1/2 cup fine, dry breadcrumbs
- 1/2 cup dry stuffing mix
- 1/2 cup crushed cornflake cereal

Combine one sauce-maker with 1 cup low-fat sour cream, 1 cup low-fat milk, 1 cup water, 1 tsp salt, and 1 tsp pepper (omit sour cream and milk when using tomatoes). Stir in the frozen vegetable, pasta/rice/potato, meat/fish/poultry, and any extras. Spoon the mixture into a 13 × 9-inch baking dish coated with cooking spray. Sprinkle with a topping. Bake the casserole covered at 350°F for 1 hour and 10 minutes. Uncover and bake for 10 more minutes or until bubbly. Yield: 6 servings.

- Eat canned and jarred goods with a high acid content (tomatoes, grapefruit, and pineapple, for example) within 18 months. Canned foods with a low acid content, such as meat, poultry, fish, and most vegetables, will keep for 2–5 years.

- Use eggs within 3 weeks of the expiration date, and keep them refrigerated at all times.

- Refrigerate fresh poultry or fish for no more than 2 days after you buy it. If it won't be used within 2 days, freeze it. Other fresh meats will keep in the fridge for up to 3–5 days.

- A food that has been cooked, served, then refrigerated within 2 hours can be stored safely in the refrigerator for 3–4 days. In the freezer, most planned-overs will store well for 2–3 months. When you store planned-overs, divide the food among small containers so that it will cool quickly. Label your storage containers with the food's name and the date it was prepared so that you'll know which items to use first.

Defrost planned-over batches of frozen foods thoroughly before cooking them. It is best not to go directly from freezer to oven, because bacteria may thrive in the center of a frozen food as the edges begin to cook. It is not safe to defrost on the kitchen counter at room temperature. Plan ahead to thaw your frozen dishes safely in the refrigerator. Use your microwave to defrost before cooking only if you will be cooking your dish immediately afterward. Microwave defrosting often cooks parts of the food, and storing partly cooked food can lead to bacteria buildup.

DAY 1 ($3.83)

Breakfast
1 orange, separated into sections ($0.33)
1 cup sugar-free, fat-free yogurt ($0.55)
2 Golden Applesauce Muffins* ($0.16)
1 cup coffee or hot tea ($0.02)

Lunch
2 cups Favorite Vegetable Soup* ($0.68)
6 saltine crackers ($0.03)
3 2-inch graham cracker squares ($0.07)
1 cup fat-free milk ($0.14)

Dinner
1 Pineapple-Glazed Ham Steak* ($0.44)
1 green salad: 2 cups lettuce, 1/4 cup grated carrot,
    5 cucumber slices ($0.41) with
2 Tbsp fat-free ranch-style dressing ($0.17)
1 cup mashed potatoes made with reduced-calorie
    margarine and fat-free milk ($0.07)
1 cup steamed broccoli florets with reduced-calorie
    margarine and lemon juice ($0.31)
1 roll ($0.08) with
1 tsp reduced-calorie margarine ($0.01)
1 Individual Cinnamon Crumb Cake* ($0.13)
12 oz iced tea ($0.02)

Snack
3/4 oz pretzels (about 7 large pretzel twists) ($0.06)
12 oz sugar-free lemonade ($0.15)

DAY 2 ($3.33)

Breakfast
1/2 cup oatmeal made with quick-cooking oats ($0.04)
    with brown sugar substitute ($0.02) and 2 Tbsp
    raisins ($0.09)

1 slice cinnamon toast (1 tsp reduced-calorie margarine,
    1/2 tsp sugar, dash cinnamon) ($0.08)
1/2 cup fat-free milk ($0.07)

Lunch
1 cup cooked spaghetti noodles ($0.10) with
1 cup Spunky Spaghetti Sauce* ($0.58)
1 Quick Garlic Bun* ($0.05)
1 No-Bake Peanut Butter Treat* ($0.14)
12 oz iced tea ($0.02)

Dinner
4 oz Golden Roasted Turkey Breast* ($0.22)
1 cup Tomato Salad Surprise* ($0.63)
1 serving Carrots, Onions, and Potatoes* ($0.20)
1/2 cup Southern-Style Green Beans* ($0.38)
1 roll ($0.08) with
1 tsp reduced-calorie margarine ($0.01)
1 serving Creamy Pumpkin Custard* ($0.23)
1 cup fat-free milk ($0.14)

Snack
3 cups air-popped popcorn ($0.05) with
2 tsp reduced-calorie margarine, melted ($0.02)
12 oz diet soda ($0.18)

DAY 3 ($6.99)

Breakfast
1 scrambled egg ($0.05)
2 slices whole-wheat toast ($0.12) with
2 tsp reduced-calorie margarine ($0.02) and
2 tsp 100% fruit spread ($0.08)
1 cup Berry and Banana Blend* ($0.50)

Lunch (Fast Food)
1 regular-size cheeseburger ($0.79)
1 small order of french fries ($0.94)

continued on next page

continued from previous page

1 side salad with fat-free dressing ($1.99)
1 small diet soda ($0.89)

Dinner
1 1/2 cups Sunday Afternoon Split Pea Soup* ($0.27)
1 square Gran's Country-Style Corn Bread* ($0.08)
1/2 cup Marinated Confetti Vegetable Salad* ($0.32)
1 square Strawberry Ribbon Supreme* ($0.54)
1 cup fat-free milk ($0.14)

Snack
1 cup Hot Chocolate with Peppermint Whipped
Topping* ($0.26)

DAY 4 ($4.55)

Breakfast
3/4 cup cornflake cereal ($0.08) with
1/2 cup fat-free milk ($0.07)
1 English muffin ($0.25) with
2 tsp reduced-calorie margarine ($0.02) and
2 tsp 100% fruit spread ($0.05)
1 cup coffee or hot tea ($0.02)

Lunch
1 turkey sandwich: 2 oz leftover Golden Roasted
    Turkey Breast,* 2 slices whole-wheat bread,
    1 tsp mustard ($0.25)
1 cup Sassy Sweet Potato Chips* ($0.29)
1 cup carrot and celery sticks ($0.10) with
2 Tbsp fat-free ranch-style dressing ($0.17)
1 apple ($0.33)
12 oz diet soda ($0.18)

Dinner
1 serving Beef and Broccoli Stroganoff* ($1.24)
Sliced tomato and cucumber (1/2 tomato,
    1/4 cucumber) ($0.40) with

2 Tbsp Tangy Dijon Vinaigrette* ($0.09)
1 slice French bread ($0.06) with
1 tsp reduced-calorie margarine ($0.01)
1 Rainbow Parfait* ($0.37)
12 oz iced tea ($0.02)

Snack
1 cup sugar-free, fat-free yogurt ($0.55)

DAY 5 ($4.23)

Breakfast
2 Banana-Oatmeal Muffins* ($0.12)
1 cup Caribbean Sunrise Smoothie* ($0.45)

Lunch
1 Gourmet Grilled Cheese* ($0.63)
3/4 oz pretzels ($0.06)
1 serving Cinnamon-Glazed Bananas* ($0.13)
12 oz diet soda ($0.18)

Dinner
1 serving Marilyn's Spicy "Fried" Chicken* ($0.56)
1 cup Cucumbers and Onions in Dill Dressing* ($0.54)
1 ear Cheesy Corn on the Cob* ($0.29)
1 cup Tasty Cooked Greens* ($0.27)
1 roll ($0.08) with
1 tsp reduced-calorie margarine ($0.01)
1 cup Spiced Raisin Bread Pudding* ($0.35)
12 oz iced tea ($0.02)

Snack
1 square leftover Strawberry Ribbon Supreme* ($0.54)

DAY 6 ($3.91)

Breakfast
1/2 cup unsweetened apple juice ($0.08)
2 slices Cinnamon French Toast* ($0.18) with

continued on next page

continued from previous page

1/4 cup Wild Berry Syrup* ($0.15)
1 cup fat-free milk ($0.14)

Lunch
2 Southwestern Chicken Wrap-Ups* ($0.84)
1 cup Sparkling Peach Spritzer* ($0.35)

Dinner
4 oz Seasoned Pan-Fried Catfish* ($0.79)
1 cup Crunchy Oriental Coleslaw* ($0.17)
1 cup Garden Vegetable Scramble* ($0.62)
1 roll ($0.08) with
1 tsp reduced-calorie margarine ($0.01)
1 serving Simple Strawberry Shortcake* ($0.30)

Snack
1 leftover Banana-Oatmeal Muffin* ($0.06)
1 cup fat-free milk ($0.14)

DAY 7 ($3.53)

Breakfast
1 cup tomato juice ($0.17)
1 Egg in a Basket* ($0.12)
2 slices crisp bacon ($0.05)
1 cup coffee or hot tea ($0.02)

Lunch
2 cups leftover Sunday Afternoon Split Pea Soup*
   ($0.36)
6 saltine crackers ($0.03)
1 slice fat-free American cheese ($0.15)
1 serving leftover Simple Strawberry Shortcake* ($0.30)
1 cup fat-free milk ($0.14)

Dinner
2 cups Tempting Turkey Pot Pie* ($0.72)
1 green salad: 2 cups lettuce, 1/4 cup grated carrot, 5
   cucumber slices ($0.41) with

2 Tbsp Tangy Dijon Vinaigrette* ($0.09)
1 Banana-Split Parfait* ($0.49)
12 oz iced tea ($0.02)

Snack
1/2 cup Creamy Apple-Cinnamon Sandwich Spread*
  ($0.40) on
1 slice whole-wheat bread ($0.06)

*Recipe included in this book.

CHAPTER 3

Cart Smarts: Shopping to Win the Grocery Store Game

The typical American household spends almost 12 cents of every dollar it earns on food. Although a portion of the money is spent on food eaten away from home, savvy supermarket shopping is one sure way to spend less and eat healthfully. Supermarkets are case studies in smart selling. In fact, grocery carts were invented because customers had a tendency to stop shopping when their baskets became too full or too heavy. This chapter will help you win the grocery store game by outlining simple shopping strategies to slash your grocery bill.

Shopping for a Supermarket

The corner market is no longer the only place to spend your food dollars. Location and convenience are important factors in selecting a store because most of us visit our supermarket at least once a week. However, it pays to know about the other options in the marketplace so that you can choose the one that offers you the most savings, based on your shopping style and priorities. A food co-op is one option for near-wholesale prices on grains, beans, and other bulk foods. But regular supermarkets, supercenters, and warehouse clubs are more commonly available.

The **regular supermarket** is the choice of almost 85% of shoppers. Everyday prices may be higher than at larger superstores, but specials and store brands are abundant. The supermarket's smaller scale means faster shopping. That can save you both time and money because more time in the grocery store usually adds up to a larger grocery bill. Surveys show that shoppers spend close to $2 for every extra minute in the market.

The **supercenter** combines a grocery store, a pharmacy, a florist, and other merchandise under one huge roof—they're often the size of six or seven typical supermarkets. Supercenters have a tremendous selection of items in most grocery categories. They tend to have low everyday prices. They also may offer to match the weekly specials found in regular supermarkets. Supercenters have many price advantages because of their size, but shopping in them is more time-consuming and challenging. Because they must be built on a large plot of undeveloped land, they are often located far from residential neighborhoods.

The **warehouse club** is a no-frills approach to food shopping. It offers minimal service, with few advertisements and a stark shopping environment. It typically charges an annual membership fee (although many provide a free 1-day pass). While the supercenter offers a wide variety of items, the warehouse club has few choices of brands or of sizes within brands. Shoppers are offered mass quantities of food, such as 5-pound boxes of crackers or cases of canned pears, at low prices. This may be a good way to stock up on staples if you have the storage space. However, a gallon tub of mayonnaise is not a good buy if it spoils before you can use it all.

Your choice of a shopping site depends on your time and savings priorities. The smartest shoppers often visit a combination of markets: the warehouse club once a month to stock up on nonperishable staples in large sizes, the supercenter to find the best everyday prices, and the regular supermarket to save time.

The regular supermarket is about 10% more expensive, but it will take half as much time to shop there. Once you select your shopping site, join the shoppers' club if your store has one. As a member, you'll receive a card that entitles you to automatic discounts or access to unadvertised, members-only specials.

Don't Leave Home without It . . .

Don't leave home for a shopping trip without planning! The smartest shoppers shrink grocery bills before they even set foot in the store.

- *Make a plan.* Use the tips in chapter 2 to plan your menus for the week based on what's on hand, leftovers, sales, and coupon/rebate items. Minimize the number of trips you make to the store each week.

- *Be a list lover.* Plan your shopping trip by making a list of what you'll need for your week's menu and stick with it! If you shop without a list, you are more apt to make impulse buys. Picking up an extra two or three items on a shopping trip can add up to $5 to $10 a week—that's $260 to $520 dollars a year! To save minutes as well as money, organize your list to match the aisle-by-aisle layout of your favorite store. Research shows that the more efficiently you make your way through the store, the less you'll spend.

- *Check out the specials.* Supermarkets frequently offer "loss leaders." These are heavily advertised low-profit items designed to lure you into the store. Check store ads and fliers for sales and specials. Keep a price notebook listing the items you buy regularly and their typical prices. Note what's on sale. Your notes will serve as a guide to the week's best buys. Shopping the specials doesn't require spending hours traveling to several stores each week. You'll find that many stores have predictable sale cycles. For example, you may be able to stock up on canned goods or boneless chicken breasts every 6 weeks, when your supermarket of choice offers them for sale.

■ *Cut costs with coupons.* Coupons are money-savers if you use them on items that you normally buy. With planning, coupons can save you between $5 and $20 for every $100 you spend on groceries. Yet less than 3% of all coupons issued are redeemed. Take the time to mail in rebate and refund offers. Trade coupons with friends.

Clip coupons and organize them in envelopes by supermarket aisle. On shopping day, select the coupons you'll need and attach them to your list. (You may also be able to clip your grocery costs without clipping coupons. Many stores now have instant coupon dispensers within easy reach of the products being discounted.) Use your coupons in combination with store sales and double/triple coupon days. For example, a store is featuring brand-name paper towels, regularly priced at $1.09, for $0.59. With a 15 cents–off coupon at a store honoring double coupons, you'll pay only $0.29 per roll. That's a savings of $0.80 per roll. Coupons don't always guarantee the best bargain, however. Many times it is still less expensive to purchase the store brand of an item than to buy a brand name with a coupon. Shop carefully!

Although the money saved by clipping coupons may not seem like much, it does add up. Using just five coupons a week at $0.50 each means a savings of $130 a year. If you need additional positive reinforcement for the time and effort it takes to clip coupons, review your weekly cash register tape and put the amount of money you saved using coupons into a jar. Put aside that cash for a special treat for yourself or your family.

■ *Ask and you shall receive.* If you like a particular product, call the toll-free consumer center number listed on its package. You'll often receive coupons for that item if you ask. Also, request that your local store start holding double or triple coupon days. Remind the manager that happy customers are repeat customers. If a sale item is sold out, ask for a rain check. Stores are required by law to provide a rain check so that you can buy the exact item at the sale price the next time you visit.

What's In Store?

It's time for your supermarket safari. Venture ahead only if you are in the proper frame of mind—it's a jungle out there! Shop alone to limit impulse buying by cranky kids and hungry spouses. Don't go when you're tired or when stores are very crowded; you'll be more concerned about getting out than about saving money. Shop after you've eaten to make the most of your willpower. Wearing a tape player or radio with headphones while you shop may also help you save. Supermarkets often play soft, soothing music to encourage you to shop slowly and therefore spend more money. Research indicates that listening to lively, upbeat music will get you out of the store faster, lowering your grocery bill.

■ **Shop with your eyes wide open.** Smart shoppers are aware of the many marketing strategies used in the grocery store. Stores are designed so that the high-traffic areas, such as the dairy and meat departments, are in the back. This means you'll have to pass through more aisles to reach them and you'll be more likely to pick up a few extra things. Foods that go together, such as chips, dips, and soft drinks, are often grouped together to encourage impulse buys. Another market strategy is to place a basic food item, such as cereal, across the aisle from an impulse item, such as candy. Cartons of merchandise stacked in the aisles also slow you down and suggest bargain pricing. Compare prices carefully before buying. Grocers place the most expensive brands and impulse items at eye level. You'll have to look on high and low shelves to find the best buys. Beware of bargains that aren't really bargains. Signs saying "new" or "special" may be eye-catching, but they do not necessarily point out low-priced items.

■ **Location, location, location.** Often, the same or similar items are sold at different prices in different parts of the store. Imported Swiss cheese at the deli counter may cost 25% more than the prepackaged store brand Swiss cheese in the dairy case. Sodas are another case in point. A 20-ounce bottle of a diet soft drink may cost $0.75 if purchased at the small refrigerator case at the checkout counter; a much larger, 2-liter bottle in the soft drink aisle may cost as little as $0.89.

- **_Don't be snobby about store brands._** Store brands or private-label items are often priced as much as 30% below their national-brand competitors. Most shoppers find store brands taste as good as brand names, which is not surprising, since the brand-name manufacturers often make the same items for the supermarket.

- **_Label Reading 101._** Use the unit price to compare the costs of different brands and package sizes. Unit price is the price per ounce, pound, or pint. Most stores show the unit price on the display shelf. Read nutrition information labels too! (See the box "Label Reading 101" at the end of this chapter.)

- **_Compare cost per edible serving._** Compare the costs of servings of different varieties of meats, fresh fruits, and vegetables. The price per pound is not always a good basis for comparing the costs of these foods because of the different amounts of bone, fat, cores, pits, skins, and other parts you can't eat. For example, after cooking, you can get three 3-ounce servings of lean meat per pound from an item with little or no fat or bone, such as round steak. However, you'll only get one serving of

BEST BUYS	BAD BUYS
■ Nonfat dry milk for baking and cooking	■ Individually wrapped, single-serving packages
■ Popcorn kernels to air pop for snacks	■ Giant boxes of low-nutrient foods
■ Large bags of plain, frozen vegetables	■ Vegetables frozen with seasonings and sauces
■ Bags of dry beans	■ Deli meat—bake a small turkey or ham yourself and slice it for sandwiches
■ Non-instant oatmeal	■ Microwavable breakfasts

lean meat per pound from an item with a greater amount of bone, gristle, and fat, such as spareribs.

■ *Is bigger better?* Buy "economy size" items only if you have space for storage and you can use them before they spoil. Large packages may not always be a better buy, particularly when a smaller-sized item has been specially priced. Also, buying in bulk may bulk you up. Studies show that people tend to eat more at each sitting when they have access to especially large packages of food.

■ *Skip the "special" food.* People with diabetes don't require special "diabetic" or "dietetic" foods. Although these products may be convenient, they are also high priced. Eat healthy foods at healthy prices, while keeping an eye on nutrient content and portion size.

■ *Money-saving markdowns.* You can save money by purchasing products that are discounted in special sale carts or damaged product bins. Check the items carefully for freshness and package condition. Pay close attention to the expiration dates on perishables. You may be pouring money down the drain if you buy a gallon of milk just before its expiration date. Shop Sunday morning for bargains on high-priced meats, such as chicken cordon bleu and stuffed breast of veal. Because these meats are often more perishable than plain meats, many stores discount them in the morning to sell them quickly.

■ *What price convenience?* If it's been grated, chopped, precooked, presliced, or individually packaged, you may be paying the price for convenience. Grated cheese typically costs more than a block of cheese you take home and grate yourself. However, in some cases convenience pays off. For example, if you only need a handful of broccoli florets for a salad, buy it from the supermarket salad bar instead of purchasing the entire head of broccoli. The premium you pay for buying salad that's washed, chopped, and bagged varies by the type of salad you're buying. A common salad of iceberg lettuce, cabbage, and carrots costs about the same whether homemade or prepackaged. A salad of more exotic

Italian-style greens, such as romaine lettuce and radicchio, costs more than twice as much packaged as it does made from scratch.

■ *Be flexible.* Although your list is your lifeline, take advantage of in-store specials by substituting them for similar foods in your meal plan. If you planned to buy grapes but find that apples are on sale, make the switch to save.

■ *At the checkout counter.* You're almost out the door, but don't forget to use the checkout counter as a last chance for additional savings opportunities. Although the accuracy rate is usually high, supermarket scanner errors can cost you money. Check your register tape before you leave. Many supermarket chains will give you the item free if the wrong price is scanned. Find out your store's policy for pricing mistakes. Also, if you pay for groceries with a debit card or a check, ask for extra cash back to save yourself a trip to the bank—and the fee that bank machines often charge.

Careful label reading is your best bet to ensure that you get the most for your nutrition dollar. The "Nutrition Facts" label lists what are known as Daily Values, which tell you how much of each kind of food should ideally be eaten in a day. Daily Values for a 2,000-calorie diet are printed on food labels, but your own nutrition needs may be higher or lower than the numbers on the label. Consult a registered dietitian for help with interpreting the food labels to meet your individual nutrition needs.

The Food and Drug Administration (FDA) now allows manufacturers to make certain claims linking the effect of a nutrient or a food to a disease or a health-related condition. Only claims supported by scientific evidence are allowed. The food used in the claim must be an adequate source of the appropriate nutrients. Two claims that relate to heart disease are of particular interest to people with diabetes:

■ "A diet low in saturated fat and cholesterol may help reduce the risk of coronary heart disease."

■ "A diet rich in fruits, vegetables, and grain products that contain fiber, particularly soluble fiber, and are low in saturated fat and cholesterol may help reduce the risk of coronary heart disease."

The following terms have been defined by the FDA and are commonly found on food labels on grocery store shelves:

■ **Free, without, no,** or **zero** means that a product contains none of the designated ingredient or only amounts that would not significantly affect the body.

• Calorie-free: fewer than 5 calories per serving

continued on next page

continued from previous page

- Cholesterol-free: 2 milligrams or less of cholesterol per serving and 2 grams or less of saturated fat per serving

- Fat-free: less than 0.5 grams of fat per serving

- Sodium-free: less than 5 milligrams of sodium per serving

- Sugar-free: less than 0.5 grams of sugar per serving

■ **Low, little, few,** and **low source of** may be used on foods that can be eaten often without exceeding the U.S. Department of Agriculture/Health and Human Services dietary guidelines.

- Low-fat: 3 grams or less of fat per serving

- Low–saturated fat: 1 gram or less of saturated fat per serving and not more than 15% of calories from saturated fat

- Low-sodium: 140 milligrams or less of sodium per serving

- Very-low-sodium: 35 milligrams or less of sodium per serving

- Low-cholesterol: 20 milligrams or less of cholesterol and 2 grams or less of saturated fat per serving

- Low-calorie: 40 calories or less per serving

■ **Lean** and **extra lean** describe the fat content of meat, poultry, and seafood.

- Lean: less than 10 grams of fat, 4.5 grams or less of saturated fat, and less than 95 milligrams of cholesterol per serving

- Extra lean: less than 5 grams of fat, less than 2 grams of saturated fat, and less than 95 milligrams of cholesterol per serving

- **High** means that the food contains 20% or more of the Daily Value for a particular nutrient per serving.

- **Good source** means that 1 serving of the food contains 10–19% of the Daily Value for a particular nutrient per serving.

- **Reduced** means that the product has been changed nutritionally and now contains at least 25% less of a given nutrient or 25% fewer calories than the regular product. However, if a product is already naturally low in that nutrient, the label can't claim that it is "reduced."

- **Less** or **fewer** means that a food contains 25% less of a nutrient or of calories than the regular product.

- **Light** has more than one meaning. A product is "light" if it contains 1/3 fewer calories or 1/2 the fat of the regular product. It can also mean that the sodium content of a low-calorie, low-fat food has been reduced by at least 50%. Finally, "light" can simply describe the product's texture and color.

- **More** on a label means that one serving of this food contains at least 10% more of the Daily Value of a nutrient than does the regular product.

- **Percent fat-free** means the product must be a low-fat or fat-free product and the percentage given must be an accurate reflection of the amount of fat present. For example, if a food contains 2.5 grams of fat per 50 grams of product, the claim must be "95% fat-free."

- **Healthy** on a label means that the food must be low in fat and saturated fat and must contain limited amounts of cholesterol and sodium. If it is a single-item food, it must provide at least 10% of the Daily

continued on next page

continued from previous page

Value for one or more of the following: vitamins A or C, iron, calcium, protein, or fiber. If it is a meal-type product, it must provide 10% of two or three of these vitamins and minerals or of protein or fiber, in addition to meeting the other criteria.

- **Fresh** means the food is raw, has never been frozen or heated, and contains no preservatives. **Fresh frozen** can be used for foods that are quickly frozen while still fresh.

CHAPTER 4

The Penny-Pincher's Food Pyramid

Eating right is an investment in your health. The better care you take of your body, the less often you'll need to visit your health care professional. The money you spend on nutritious groceries is tiny compared to today's rising medical costs.

As you learned in chapter 1, people with diabetes don't require expensive "special" foods or exotic ingredients to meet their nutrition goals. To stay healthy, you need to eat the proper amount of each type of food every day. Following the USDA Food Guide Pyramid or the Diabetes Food Pyramid from *The First Step in Diabetes Meal Planning* will help you make the good food choices that are essential to your diabetes care.

Both pyramids are guides to good eating. However, the Diabetes Food Pyramid is more focused on diabetes meal planning than the USDA Food Guide Pyramid. Both pyramids have six sections. The fruit and vegetable categories are the same. But the other categories have the following slight differences:

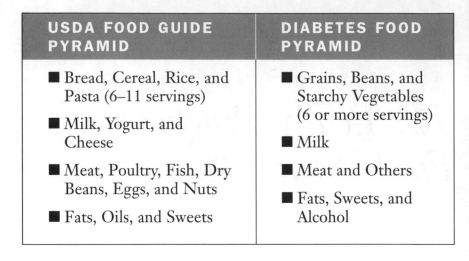

USDA FOOD GUIDE PYRAMID	DIABETES FOOD PYRAMID
■ Bread, Cereal, Rice, and Pasta (6–11 servings) ■ Milk, Yogurt, and Cheese ■ Meat, Poultry, Fish, Dry Beans, Eggs, and Nuts ■ Fats, Oils, and Sweets	■ Grains, Beans, and Starchy Vegetables (6 or more servings) ■ Milk ■ Meat and Others ■ Fats, Sweets, and Alcohol

Some foods are listed in different groups. In the USDA Food Guide Pyramid, dry beans are in the meat group, and cheese is in the milk group. But in the Diabetes Food Pyramid, dry beans are in the group with grains, and cheese is in the meat group. The USDA Food Guide Pyramid does not mention alcohol, but it is included in the tip of the Diabetes Food Pyramid. Both pyramids suggest that you should limit your intake of items from the category at the tip.

This chapter is a guide to penny-pinching and best buys in all sections of the food pyramid as it appears in *The First Step in Diabetes Meal Planning*. Grab your grocery cart and calculator to start saving your money—and your health!

Grains, Beans, and Starchy Vegetables

The foods in this group are the foundation of an inexpensive, healthy meal plan. They are low in cost, low in fat (unless prepared with added fat), and generally high in fiber. Eat 6 or more servings from this group every day, depending on your specific meal plan.

Best Buys

Cornmeal
Flour

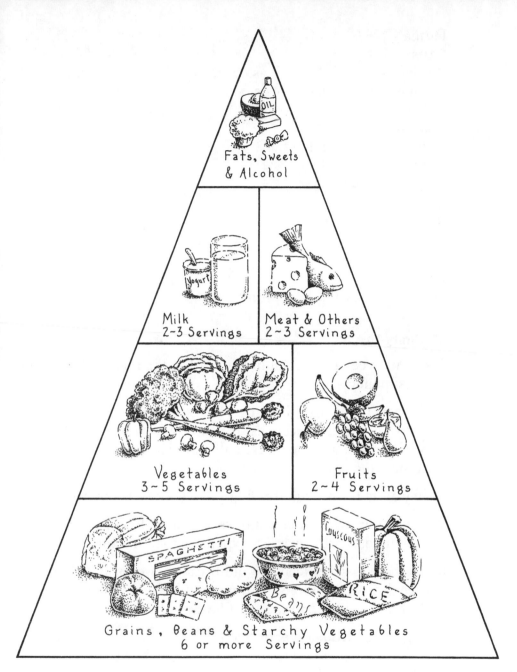

Diabetes Food Pyramid

Farina

Grits

Ready-to-eat cereals, such as corn, wheat, and bran flakes;
   puffed rice and oat cereals; and shredded wheat

Rolled oats

Bread

Hamburger or hot dog buns

Saltines

Popcorn kernels

Dry beans

Rice

Pasta

Corn

Potatoes

Sweet potatoes and yams, fresh

$$ Thrifty Tips $$

■ Buy unsweetened cereal in bags rather than boxes. Packaging
costs money.

■ Try generic or store-brand cereals to save 20–30% over the
cost of brand-name cereals. If you find it hard to make the
switch, mix a generic cereal half and half with a brand name
of the same type to extend your savings.

■ Stay away from single-serving packets or boxes of cereals.

■ Cook your own hot cereal to save money. Regular or quick-
cooking oats are much less expensive than instant oats.

■ Purchase lower-priced day-old bread to use for breadcrumbs,
French toast, croutons, stuffing, and bread pudding. Day-old
pound cake is fine to use for a layered fruit trifle dessert.

■ Rolls made from a mix or from dough found in the dairy
case are cheaper and tastier than packaged or bakery rolls.

■ Instead of an expensive ready-made pizza crust, buy frozen
bread dough, thaw it, and roll it out for a low-cost pizzeria
taste.

■ Beans have been called "poor man's meat" because they are
an excellent alternative to meat, at only pennies per pound.

- Dry beans triple in volume when they're soaked and cooked. A 1-pound bag will make six 1-cup servings.

- Blended bean mixes and gourmet beans are almost three times as expensive as bean mix you make yourself.

- Canned and frozen beans are also good buys, and they save you time as well.

- Instant, quick-cooking, and seasoned rice mixes cost almost three times more than plain rice that you cook and season yourself.

- For convenience, buy regular rice, cook more than you need, and freeze the extra for future use.

- Pasta is cheaper when purchased in bags rather than boxes.

- Pasta shapes are interchangeable in recipes. Choose the least expensive pasta and substitute it for a more expensive variety of a similar size and shape:
  - Long, thin noodles: fettuccine, linguine, spaghetti, spaghettini, vermicelli
  - Twisted and curved pasta: cavatappi, elbow macaroni, farfalle, fusilli, orecchiette, radiatore, rotelle, seashell macaroni
  - Tube-shaped pasta: mostaccioli, penne, rigatoni, ziti
  - Small tube- or rice-shaped pasta: orzo, tubetti

- Compare the prices of different forms of the same starchy vegetable. If you plan to mash sweet potatoes and the price for fresh is almost the same as the price for canned, buy the canned sweet potatoes. They will require less preparation time, and you won't be paying for the peelings.

- Check the drained weight of a can of corn. Frozen corn may be more economical.

- Potatoes are less expensive if purchased in 10-pound bags.

Vegetables

Vegetables are naturally low in fat and calories and are a great source of vitamins and minerals. Eat at least 3–5 servings per day, according to your specific meal plan.

Best Buys

Bean sprouts, fresh	Green beans	Onions
Cabbage	Kale	Sauerkraut
Carrots	Lettuce	Turnip greens, canned
Celery	Mustard greens	Tomatoes, canned
Cucumbers		

$$ Thrifty Tips $$

■ Simpler is smarter. Vegetables frozen in butter sauce cost twice as much as plain frozen vegetables—and they have more calories too!

■ If you are purchasing bagged fresh vegetables, weigh a few bags and choose the heaviest. There may be as much as a 3/4 pound difference between two "5-pound" bags of onions.

■ Use marked-down vegetables for soups, stews, and stir-fry.

■ If the cost of lettuce is too high, use cabbage or other leafy greens (such as collard greens, turnip greens, kale, spinach, and Swiss chard) to make salads.

■ When buying fresh greens by weight, be sure to shake off the excess water before you put them in your cart. It's amazing how much water can be hidden in the leaves.

■ Bagged, fresh spinach will give you more for your money because it contains fewer stems.

■ Be careful before paying extra money for "organic" vegetables. Currently, there are no federal standards for regulation or testing to ensure that these vegetables are free of chemical fertilizers, pesticides, or preservatives. New regulations are expected to set tougher standards. Don't pay high prices for vegetables that still contain chemical additives.

■ Fresh vegetables "in season" are a best buy. You may want to buy extras and freeze them to use throughout the year. Economical and nutritious choices in the winter include turnips, carrots, and cabbage.

■ If fresh vegetables are too expensive, use frozen or canned. Pour just the amount you need from a 1-pound bag of frozen vegetables, then twist-tie and refreeze the remainder for later use. Canned vegetables contain the same nutritional value, but may be lower priced. If sodium is a concern, rinse and drain the vegetables before using them, but keep in mind that you may be rinsing away some nutrients.

■ Make your own tomato sauce and save. Just simmer canned tomatoes with green peppers, onions, and spices until thick.

■ Convenience costs money. One pound of carrots may cost about $0.69, but a bag of pre-shredded carrots may be priced at $1.29 for 10 ounces—almost $2.06 per pound! Celery hearts may be $1.69 per pound versus $0.79 for a pound of whole celery stalks. Shred your own cabbage for coleslaw instead of buying it pre-shredded.

■ Remember to consider the edible weight of vegetables. Different vegetables yield a different number of servings per pound; for example, 5–6 servings per pound of green beans, 4–5 servings per pound of Brussels sprouts, and 3–4 servings per pound of broccoli.

■ For the most economical vegetables, grow your own! See chapter 5.

Fruits

Fruits are a good source of vitamins, minerals, and fiber. They are sweet tasting and fat free—a winning combination when a snack attack hits! Eat at least 2–4 servings daily, according to your individual meal plan.

Best Buys

Apples	Oranges	Pears, fresh	Applesauce
Bananas	Grapefruit	Tangerines	

Fruit juices, including orange, grapefruit, apple, grape, pineapple, and prune

$$ Thrifty Tips $$

■ Apples and oranges cost less when bought by the bag rather than individually. Snack on the perfect pieces and use the less-than-perfect ones for apple crisp or fruit salad.

■ Fresh fruits "in season" are always a good buy. Economical choices, even in the winter, are apples, pears, bananas, and citrus fruits, such as oranges, grapefruits, and tangerines.

■ If fresh fruit is too expensive, buy frozen or canned fruit. Rinse heavy syrup off canned fruits if you are concerned about carbohydrate content.

■ Buy fresh berries on sale. Freeze them on a cookie sheet, and then store them in plastic bags in the freezer to use year-round.

■ Price fruits with an eye to the cost per edible serving. If you are paying by the pound, you will be paying for the inedible seeds and rind of cantaloupe, for example.

■ Avoid shopping for fruit and other produce on Sunday evening, when stock is low and the new bounty has yet to arrive.

■ Think twice about buying expensive "organically grown" fruits. Ideally, organic fruits are cleaner, safer, and closer to nature. But until national standards governing the use of the word "organic" are in place, you may be getting less than you're paying for.

■ Frozen concentrated juice is a better buy than cartons or jars of reconstituted juice or juice boxes.

■ Mix canned fruit with fresh seasonal fruit for a low-cost fruit cup.

Milk

Dive into dairy foods, such as milk and yogurt, for a rich source of calcium and many vitamins and minerals. Select 2–3 servings a day from the dairy group, depending on your specific meal plan.

Best Buys

Fat-free milk   Nonfat dry milk

$$ Thrifty Tips $$

- Use nonfat dry milk for cooking and baking. It is inexpensive and has a long shelf life.

- Although you shouldn't buy more milk than you can safely use before the expiration date, a gallon is usually more economical than a quart or a half gallon. Check the unit price to be sure.

- If you only need a small amount of buttermilk in a recipe, don't buy a whole quart. Make "sour" milk by stirring 1 tablespoon of lemon juice or vinegar into enough milk to equal 1 cup. Let the mixture stand for 5 minutes, then use it as you would buttermilk.

- Instead of buying small containers of yogurt, buy a quart and separate it into 1-cup servings yourself.

- Make fruit or flavored yogurt by adding your own fruit to plain yogurt. It's a better buy and better nutrition.

- Substitute evaporated milk (not fat-free milk) for more expensive whipped cream in an aerosol can. Whip the evaporated milk yourself using an ice-cold bowl and an electric mixer.

Meat and Others

Americans spend 16 cents of every food dollar on meat, so significant food savings can be found in this part of the pyramid.

In the Diabetes Food Pyramid, this group contains meats of all types and other protein foods, such as cheese, seafood, eggs, and peanut butter. Two to three servings of 2–3 ounces each are recommended every day as a good source of protein as well as certain vitamins and minerals.

Best Buys

Ground beef
Beef chuck roast
Beef chuck steak
Fresh pork: Boston butt and shoulder
Cured pork: picnic and ham
Turkey: whole or drumsticks
Chicken: whole, wings, or drumsticks
Dry beans
Dry peas
Eggs
Peanut butter
Tuna, canned
Pasteurized processed cheese
Pasteurized processed cheese spread and cheese food
Some natural cheese, including brick, mozzarella, and cheddar

$$ Thrifty Tips $$

■ Control meat portion size to control costs, as well as cholesterol and saturated fat. The correct serving size for meat is 2–3 ounces. That's the size of the palm of a woman's hand or a deck of cards.

■ Make meat a side dish instead of the centerpiece of the meal. Smaller servings of meat mean bigger savings on your grocery bill.

■ Use less meat than is called for in a recipe. Often the amount called for can be reduced by one-fourth and not be missed. Use extra beans, rice, or pasta to extend the meat in soups, stews, and chili. Substitute thawed, chopped frozen spinach for half of the cheese or meat in a lasagna.

- Try meatless meals several times a week. Use low-cost sources of protein, such as eggs, peanut butter, or dry beans. One egg, 1/4 cup of egg substitute, 2 egg whites, 2 table-spoons of peanut butter, or 1/2 cup of cooked dry beans is the protein equivalent of 1 ounce of meat.

- The least expensive cuts of meat are pork loin roast, boneless loin chops, boneless cooked ham, beef round, sirloin tip, and rump roast. Low fat content means less shrinkage and waste during cooking.

- Boneless cuts of meat are often better buys, since you aren't paying for the weight of the bone. Think in terms of cost per edible serving rather than strictly cost per pound. Turkey has 46% edible meat per pound, while chicken has 41% edible meat per pound.

- Avoid value-added meats, such as pre-marinated flank steak. Buy flank steak by the pound and marinate it yourself. Use an inexpensive reduced-fat or fat-free Italian vinaigrette salad dressing instead of a package or bottle of marinade.

- Don't use expensive cuts of meat in stews or casseroles.

- Use less meat and more lettuce, tomatoes, and vegetables on sandwiches. Deli meat may be less expensive than pre-packaged lunchmeats. Buy a small cooked ham and have the deli slice it thinly. Another alternative is to bake a small turkey breast or ham yourself and slice it thinly for sandwiches.

- Buy whole chickens on sale. Bone and skin the chicken yourself. Cut it and put it into individual packages of legs, breasts, thighs, and backs to use as your recipes and your family's taste require. Remember that drumsticks have a lower ratio of meat to bone and skin, so their edible portion costs are higher.

- Wait for a sale, stock up, and then freeze boneless chicken breasts. You can get four servings per pound of chicken when you use it as part of a stir-fry.

- Make your own chicken tenders: Pound a boneless chicken breast to 1/2 inch thickness. Then cut it into strips using kitchen shears.

- Tuna, salmon, and sardines canned in water, tomato sauce, or mustard are low-cost fish catches.

- Ask for fish scraps at the fish counter in your grocery store. The scraps make wonderful chowders and soups.

- Skip the store-made tuna or crab salad. It takes very little time and money to make it yourself. Making it at home will also allow you to keep the fat content low.

- Serve breakfast for dinner occasionally. A very economical omelet can be made with eggs, leftover vegetables, and cooked potatoes.

- There is no nutritional difference between brown and white eggs. Choose white eggs since they cost less.

- If there is less than 7 cents' difference between two sizes of the same grade of eggs, choose the larger egg for better value.

- Why buy expensive egg substitutes? Two egg whites can replace one egg in a recipe. Two egg whites mixed with one whole egg can be substituted for two eggs.

- Save money by buying a block of cheese and grating it yourself.

- Use small amounts of strong-flavored cheeses, such as Parmesan or sharp cheddar, rather than large amounts of milder cheeses. You'll save money and fat calories.

Fats, Sweets, and Alcohol

The foods at the tip of the pyramid should be eaten sparingly. Fats add flavor, but also calories. There is no suggested number of fat servings each day, but you should stay close to the number of grams or servings in your meal plan. Sweets are no longer off-limits for people with diabetes. They can be eaten occasionally, in small amounts, as long as they are substituted for other carbohydrates and as long as you know how they affect your blood glucose. Alcohol has no nutrients and should be limited. The items in this section of the pyramid are mostly impulse purchases that are expensive for your health and your pocketbook. They add calories, but little or no nutrition for the money you spend. Use these foods wisely, to add variety, but not to replace more nutritious foods.

$$ Thrifty Tips $$

■ Make your own nonstick cooking spray by putting vegetable oil in a spray bottle.

■ Olive oil is available in several grades. Use the costly extra virgin olive oil in cold dishes where its taste is apparent, such as salad dressings. Use a less expensive grade, such as virgin olive oil, in spicy dishes or dishes that will be heated.

■ Greek or Spanish olive oil may be a better buy than Italian.

■ Small bags of shelled walnuts, pecans, and almonds are costly. Buy a large bag on sale around the holidays and keep it in the freezer to use in cooking year-round. Buy loose nuts by the pound for even more savings.

■ Special "diabetic" or "dietetic" foods are no bargain. Case in point:

Fructose-sweetened chocolate sandwich cookies
3 cookies = 160 calories, 7 grams fat, 26 grams carbohydrate
Cost = $0.35

Regular chocolate sandwich cookies
3 cookies = 140 calories, 5 grams fat, 23 grams carbohydrate
Cost = $0.13

Be a smart shopper!

■ Make your own frozen juice bars by pouring juice into small paper cups to freeze. Insert a Popsicle stick into each cup when the juice is partially frozen.

■ Rather than buying individual packages of pudding, make your own small servings from instant pudding mix and fat-free milk.

Pyramid Penny-Pinching Saves Over 40%!

Typical List		*Smart Shopper List*	
Instant Oatmeal 12 packets	$3.45	Quick Cooking Oats 12 servings	$1.93
Lima Beans (frozen in butter) 10-oz package	$1.45	Lima Beans (frozen plain) 10-oz package	$0.71
Red Delicious Apples (loose) 5 lb	$2.97	Red Delicious Apples (bagged) 5 lb	$1.99
Strawberry Fat-Free Yogurt 8 oz	$0.89	Plain Fat-Free Yogurt with Fresh Strawberries 8 oz	$0.51
Shredded Cheddar Cheese 8 oz	$2.75	Block Cheddar Cheese 8 oz	$1.65
Marinated Pork Tenderloin 1 lb	$5.99	Plain Pork Tenderloin 1 lb	$3.99
Brand-Name Extra Virgin Olive Oil 8.5 oz	$4.99	Store-Brand Extra Virgin Olive Oil 8.5 oz	$2.99
"Lite" Microwave Popcorn 8 servings	$2.49	Plain Popcorn (to air pop) 8 servings	$0.36
TOTAL	**$24.98**		**$14.13**

Prices obtained from Krogers, Lexington, KY, June 1998.

- Two economical and healthy alternatives to sweet rolls and doughnuts are cinnamon toast made with your own home-made mix of cinnamon and sugar, and fruit spread or fruit butter on whole wheat toast, English muffins, or bagels. Try "Apple-Prune Spread" on page 118!

- A tablespoon of flavored liqueur is an alternative topping for fruit salad or frozen yogurt.

Miscellaneous

$$ Thrifty Tips $$

Beverages

- Sodas, carbonated fruit drinks, and flavored waters are poor choices for both nutritional and economical reasons. Use water as your main beverage and watch your food costs drop. Add a slice of lemon, lime, or orange for fruit taste and a twist of color.

- Make your own combination juice drinks. It is cheaper to mix two juices together rather than purchase a premixed bottle of juce, such as cranberry-apple.

- Beverages packed in sports bottles are premium priced.

- Bottled tea, canned tea, or instant tea mix is far more expensive than tea made from tea bags. When purchasing tea, figure the cost based on the number of quarts you'll be able to make rather than on the weight of the jar or box.

- Add a bit of ground cinnamon or a few drops of almond or vanilla extract to coffee grounds before brewing to make your own flavored coffee.

Herbs

- Generic brands of herbs and spices can cost 50% less than brand names.

- Buy small amounts of less frequently used dried herbs and spices.

- Fresh herbs such as marjoram, oregano, rosemary, savory, and thyme freeze well.

- Start your own herb garden! See chapter 5.

Snacks

- Pass on pricey low-fat cookies and chips. Low-fat doesn't always mean healthy or low-calorie.

- Avoid individually packaged snacks. The cost of a single-serving bag of potato chips works out to over $5 per pound! Use carrot or celery sticks for crunch in lunch instead. Or try homemade chips, like the "Sassy Sweet Potato Chips" found on p. 87, for variety.

- Penny-pinching healthy snacks include

  Air-popped popcorn
  Unsalted pretzels
  Animal crackers
  Graham crackers
  Fresh fruit
  Raw vegetables
  Applesauce
  Unsweetened ready-to-eat cereal

CHAPTER 5

How Does Your Garden Grow?

Gardening is not a dirty word if you want to spend less and eat healthfully. In recent years, many people have stopped raising food in their own backyards because of lack of time or space. However, the bountiful benefits of gardening make it worth a second look.

Growing a garden is good for your wallet. For the price of a few starter plants or packets of seeds, you can enjoy fresh herbs or vegetables for months. Canning and freezing the fruits of your harvest ensures year-round savings. A stroll through your backyard garden, picking crisp green beans or juicy tomatoes for supper, or a look at your well-stocked pantry shelf and freezer beats a harried trip to the produce aisle of your local grocery store any time.

Gardening is work, but the physical activity it requires is an added benefit for people with diabetes, particularly those with type 2 diabetes who are trying to increase their physical activity and reach a desirable body weight. The short list of sample gardening activities in Table 1 notes the calories burned per hour by a 150-pound person and lists the muscle groups used.

Although gardening does require an investment of time, it can be a great stress-buster. The outdoor setting, physical activity, and sense of satisfaction from seeing the results of hard work

TABLE 1

Gardening Activity	Calories Used per Hour	Muscles Used
Planting seeds/plants	273	Arms, especially biceps and triceps
Pushing a wheelbarrow	341	Large muscle groups in the legs, especially quadriceps and hamstrings
Pulling weeds	307	Full-body workout

bring peace of mind to many Americans who enjoy gardening as a hobby.

This chapter only peeks into the possibilities of gardening for fun and savings. Abundant resources are available through your local library, your state's Cooperative Extension Service office (listed under "County Government" in your telephone directory), and the Internet. Delve into gardening to create a dirt cheap grocery bill!

Harvesting Herbs

An herb garden is a wonderful place to begin perfecting your gardening skills. Herbs provide color, texture, and inviting aroma. They are versatile plants, used in a variety of ways from herb teas and jellies to flavored vinegars and oils for marinades, salad dressings, and sauces. Herbs are relatively easy to grow, whether on a sunny windowsill, in an outdoor container, or on a plot of backyard land.

Indoor Gardening

Windowsill herb gardening can be done with year-round favorites such as oregano, chives, mint, rosemary, and thyme.

Specific growing information for each herb variety is available where you buy your starter plants, but the following general guidelines will help you get growing. Select the sunniest window you have. Herbs require at least 6 hours of sunlight a day for the best development of their flavors. (Oregano is a particularly light-loving plant.) Your windowsill must be at least 5 inches wide to safely hold a 4-inch pot with a drainage saucer, the ideal size for beginning gardeners. Select small herb plants for starters, and transplant them into a premium-quality commerical potting mix in terra-cotta pots with plastic liners or rubber pads to catch leaks. Small containers require more frequent watering, especially since heated air indoors tends to dry plants out quickly. Check your plants every day, keeping the potting mix evenly moist by watering with a light spray. Remember: Every watering leaches nutrients from the soil, so use a liquid feed to replace what has been washed away.

Leaves can be picked at any time of year, but for the best flavor, herbs should be harvested after their flower buds have formed and before they burst into bloom. Harvest your herbs in the morning, when their oils are at their strongest. Cut only what you'll need to use for the day, handling the leaves carefully. Use sharp scissors to avoid bruising and loss of flavorful oils. Fresh herbs should enhance the flavor of food, not overwhelm it. Snip leaves with scissors, adding herbs to hot food at the last minute so that they retain texture and color. Cold dishes benefit from a sprinkling of herbs several hours before serving, or even overnight, to fully develop their flavor. A good rule of thumb is to use 1 tablespoon of fresh herbs to equal 1 teaspoon of crushed dried herbs in a recipe. Although herbs taste best when fresh from the garden, drying or freezing them will preserve any extras for future use.

The Great Outdoors

If you have a bit more ambition and square-footage, herbs can be grown outdoors in either a container or a garden plot. Container herb gardens, such as those grown in a half-barrel, are popular in cooler climates because they can be moved inside easily during cold snaps. Herbs can become part of an existing vegetable garden or can be grown in their own small bed. A 4 × 6-foot space should easily accommodate a variety of herbs such as basil, cilantro, mint, oregano, parsley, rosemary, sage, tarragon, and thyme. The same general tips for growing indoor herbs apply to those grown in containers or outdoor gardens, but there are some special considerations.

Your local climate is the main influence on the variety of herbs you choose to grow. Most herbs will grow in all parts of the U.S., but the country is divided into 11 regions, or growing zones, dependent upon factors such as rainfall, sunshine, and temperature. Your state's Cooperative Extension Service will have complete information about your growing zone and which plants are most compatible with it.

Soil quality is also key. Some experts suggest that an herb garden bed be raised 10 or more inches off the ground for the best drainage. The soil should be a mixture of sterilized topsoil, peat moss, and sand or fine gravel. Testing the soil's pH is also a good idea; herbs thrive in a slightly acidic or near-neutral pH. Your county extension service can also provide you with information on soil testing in your area.

Choose a sunny location for your garden and design it so that the perennial herbs (such as mint, oregano, rosemary, sage, tarragon, and thyme) are placed first. Then fill in the garden with annuals (such as basil and cilantro) and perhaps a biennial (such as parsley). Smaller herbs, such as oregano, parsley, and creeping thyme, belong in the front of the southern-facing exposure of your garden so that the taller plants, such as basil, tarragon, and cilantro, do not shade them. Allow plenty of space for herbs to grow. In general, 18 inches between plants should be sufficient.

Finding the right watering plan for your outdoor herb garden may be a challenge. Herbs prefer dry soil, so they need only about an inch of water per week. Experienced gardeners use the soup-can trick to measure the amount of water their plants are receiving. Place several soup cans among your herbs before you turn on your hose and note the time it takes to reach an inch of water in the cans. Use that as your guide for the proper watering time in the future. Water your herbs in the morning to give them time to dry out and to prevent fungus growth. Just as good record keeping is important for your diabetes control, so is a diary of your herb-growing experiences important for your herb garden's success. Note your successes and failures, complete with details on location, watering, and fertilizing to ensure a better harvest in the future.

Hitting Pay Dirt in Your Kitchen Garden

Raising food in the backyard was once a matter of survival. Most of us no longer live off the land, but homegrown produce does help to lower grocery costs. The best advice for a novice gardener is to start small and to think carefully about what you would like to plant. Your most valuable resource is your time. Spending hours toiling and tilling a plot of potatoes is not an economical use of your time if 10 pounds of potatoes are available at the grocery store for $1.68. Plan ahead to grow just the amount of produce you're able to consume, preserve, and store to avoid wasting time and resources. Your kitchen garden should be based on actual past grocery-store purchases of fruits and vegetables.

A productive vegetable garden of beans, beets, carrots, corn, cucumbers, lettuce, onions, peppers, tomatoes, and zucchini can be raised in a plot of land as small as 10 × 15 feet. The key elements of gardening—soil, water, sunlight, and seed—remain the same no matter what the site. Your soil quality will be enhanced if you add organic matter, compost, and a balanced, natural fertilizer. Raised beds are recommended for easy reach and the most yield per square foot. Select a site close to your water source to save time and water. To receive maximum sun exposure, your garden should be set up so that the beds run from east to west.

The source of your garden plants is another place for savings. Fruits such as berries may be started from cuttings from existing plants. Most vegetables can be purchased in flats of seedlings from a nursery or garden center. Corn, carrots, beets, and beans are best started from seeds directly in the garden. Bargains on vegetable seeds can be found if you catalog-shop or buy your seeds at season's end in a local store and hold them in a cool, dry place until the following year. Join a local garden club to tap into a wonderful source of advice as well as perfectly good plants you get from other members at plant swaps and sales. As always, the resources of your county extension service, the library, and the Internet are available for more specific advice on your garden situation.

If a large garden plot is beyond the limits of your time and talents, a mini kitchen garden as small as 5 × 7 feet grown on a patio or balcony may be your solution. Lettuce, tomatoes, peppers, and eggplants adapt well to life in the concrete jungle if they are potted properly. Zucchini, snap beans, and cucumbers are other possibilities. Some varieties of cherry tomatoes can be grown in hanging baskets if they are cared for carefully. Put your windowsill to use and sprout pots of herbs or jars of seeds for future use.

From Plot to Pot and In Between

Although the fruits of your garden taste best when freshly picked, it is also economical to store them for future use. There are a variety of storage methods available. The easiest and least expensive is the old-fashioned root cellar; carrots, potatoes, and onions do well here. However, many modern gardeners don't have the space for this method. Fruits can be dehydrated into snacks. If you don't want to make the investment in a food dehydrator, sun drying, air-drying, or drying in a low-temperature oven are other alternatives. Remember that dried fruits are concentrated sources of fructose (fruit sugar), and their serving size in exchange lists and carbohydrate counting portions is usually quite small, approximately 1/4 cup.

Home canning works for preserving almost everything in your garden, but it requires attention to many details, including pH levels, bacteria, processing time, and proper seals. Consult your county extension agent for information on the latest and safest canning methods. Although a freezer is not a small investment, it can pay for itself over time with the money saved by preserving your harvest bounty. Some vegetables and fruits freeze better than others do. Vegetables freeze best if blanched (cooked in boiling water for a very short time) first so that they retain their color, flavor, and texture. Fruits can be packed and frozen in water, apple juice, or syrup. Reusable freezer containers are the least expensive way to store your harvest for future use.

Finally, even if you don't have a green thumb, you can reap the money-saving benefits of gardening by looking for the "pick your own" farms and farmers' markets in your area. According to the U.S. Department of Agriculture, nearly a million people visit farmers' markets every week for low-cost, high-quality produce. Take advantage of Mother Nature for penny-wise produce!

CHAPTER 6

Eating Out on a Lean Budget

I t's 4 o'clock in the afternoon. Maybe it has been a long day at work and you're tired. Maybe you're facing a busy evening of church, club, or children's activities. Maybe you've been under stress and need a treat. These are the times when you are most likely to say, "I can't even think about cooking tonight." If you do, you certainly won't be alone. In fact, 44 cents of every food dollar is spent on food prepared away from home, whether it be from a fast-food restaurant, carryout, or home delivery.

Does managing your diabetes meal plan on a budget mean an end to eating out? Of course not! As you can see from the meal plans in chapter 2, it is possible to eat away from home and still spend less than $7 a day on food. You must learn to eat out economically, since it's likely you'll be eating away from home even more frequently in the future. Industry experts predict a rise in restaurant dining as consumers look for ways to eat well on busy days. Careful planning on your part will prevent dining out from taking a big bite out of your budget.

Savings Strategies

Savings strategies for eating out can make a big dollar difference, especially if you consider that the average American eats at least four meals away from home weekly and spends over $681 dollars a year doing it. Keep these tips in mind when you mull over your dining-out options:

- ■ *Face the figures.* Take a careful look at the amount of money you currently spend on food prepared away from home. Save your receipts, and track the amount you spend in a typical month. It may convince you to alter your eating habits. Dining away from home is an expensive convenience. Just one fast-food "value meal" can be more expensive than an entire day's worth of healthy foods you prepare yourself.

- ■ *Good health is your best investment.* Eating right for your diabetes is a blue-chip investment. It is often difficult to find nutritious—and economical—choices on the road. Invest in one of the several helpful books that have been written on the subject, such as *The American Diabetes Association Guide to Healthy Restaurant Eating* by Hope S. Warshaw. You will be surprised to find that many strategies for eating healthfully in restaurants are also good for your piggy bank.

- ■ *Plan ahead.* Try not to eat out impulsively. Think first about the planned-over meals you have ready at home. It may take just as much time to wait in a fast-food drive-through line as it would to microwave a much healthier pre-plated meal in your own kitchen. The savings are significant!

No matter which dining-out option you choose, remember:

- ■ *A little knowledge goes a long way.* You'll want to make smart nutrition choices, no matter which menu you're ordering from. Ask for nutrition information from the restaurants you eat at often. Many chains have pamphlets with all the facts and figures you need. And all restaurants making nutrition claims for menu items, such as "low fat" or "heart healthy," must back them up with the same definitions the government requires for food labels in the grocery store. (See chapter 3.) For example, a "heart healthy" menu item will indicate that a diet low in saturated fat and cholesterol may reduce the risk of heart disease.

- **Share.** Restaurants are notorious for their oversized portions. Take advantage of this by sharing with a dining companion. For example, one person would order a large salad and the other a traditional entrée, such as a chicken dish, with side items. Share your meals for better portion control and less expense.

- **Take it home.** Another way to turn oversized restaurant portions to your advantage is to take home the leftovers. Ask for a "to go" container as your meal is being served. If you pack up half of your entrée right away, you won't be tempted to eat it all. You'll stay closer to the amount of food your body needs, as well as save money by having tomorrow's lunch or dinner "in the bag." Be sure to follow the food safety rules noted later in this chapter.

Make It Fast

It's very likely you will dash into a fast-food restaurant, grab a take-out meal from a grocery store, or order food to be delivered to your home sometime this week. In any given month, 70% of U.S. households make at least one carryout food purchase. Here are some helpful hints:

- **When is a value meal not a value?** When it contains more food than you need to stick with your meal plan! If you want to order from the value menu, share your meal with a friend or family member to get the most for your money—and your health.

- **Super-size isn't always wise.** You may be getting more food for your extra $0.39, but you are also piling on an extra 330 calories, 16 grams of fat, and 215 milligrams of sodium from french fries alone! If you must get the super-size, share your order with your dining companions.

- **Keep it simple.** Stick with foods in their simplest forms. A grilled chicken sandwich is cheaper and generally lower in fat and calories than the "deluxe" version. Eat like a child. The menu items marked "plain," "small," and "regular" are the best for your budget and your health.

- **Sub shopping.** Order a large version of your favorite healthy submarine sandwich and save half for another meal. The 12-inch size is often a better value than two 6-inch subs, and you'll benefit from the planned-overs tomorrow.

- **Chicken?** When carrying out from a chicken restaurant or grocery store rotisserie display, order a whole chicken and several side items rather than individual boxed meals for your family. You will be better able to control your portion sizes and extend your meal. Use leftover chicken scraps for soups or casseroles.

- **Pizza party.** Always use coupons or ask for today's specials over the telephone. Pizza makes great planned-overs for future meals. Set aside your extra slices immediately to avoid the "just one more bite" syndrome.

- **Beverage bargains.** Water is always your best bet as a beverage choice—and it's free! Fat-free milk and juices give you more nutrition bang for your buck than do sodas or tea.

Have a Seat

Surely it must have been a burned-out cook who said, "I'm making my favorite thing for dinner tonight—a reservation!" Getting out of the kitchen to enjoy a restaurant meal can be the highlight of the week. Use these hints to enjoy your meal and stay within your food budget.

- **Choose a restaurant for taste—and savings—appeal.** Eating in ethnic restaurants can be fun and inexpensive. For example, Chinese food is based on low-cost ingredients and cooking styles, so menu prices are reasonable. Food is often served family style, and sharing of dishes is encouraged—money saving strategies you'll love. Go meatless occasionally. Vegetarian restaurants offer healthful, low-cost entrées.

Neighborhood restaurants may be less expensive than national chains.

- **Time your dining.** Beat the clock by going to restaurants that offer early-bird specials. Also note that the very same menu items are often less expensive at lunch than at dinner. Portion sizes are more reasonable too. Breakfast items may be your best budget bet, no matter what time of day.

- **"Specials" aren't always less expensive.** Listen carefully as the specials for the day are described, and don't be afraid to ask their prices. Although you may think the word "special" means money-saving, it may be used to note the chef's specialty dish. There is no guarantee that it will be less expensive than the regular menu items.

- **Avoid alcohol and appetizers.** Alcohol quickly adds up on your restaurant tab. Consider that you could buy a case of wine for what some restaurants charge for a bottle. Don't fill up on appetizers if you plan to order an entrée and side dishes. Do you really need the calories or the expense?

- **Make creative meal choices.** Don't feel obliged to order an entrée for each person at the table. Why not make more creative and inexpensive meal choices? For example, order a side salad for a starter and make an appetizer your main course. Or eat family style: order a few entrées for the table and share them with your dining companions.

- **Dessert dilemma?** Often, you just want a "taste of something sweet" at the end of a restaurant meal. A good approach for your diabetes and your budget is to order one dessert (with extra forks!) to share with everyone at the table. Try flavored decaffeinated coffee for another inexpensive sweet treat.

- **Is a dining card program for you?** Discount dining cards or programs through credit card companies may save you 20–50% in participating restaurants if you're a frequent diner. Investigate several programs before becoming a member. There may be an annual fee for joining and special requirements for obtaining discounts.

Keep It Safe

Handle take-out foods and leftovers with care. They're no bargain if you suffer from foodborne illness. Top tips include:

■ For hot foods, pick up food while it's very hot, and eat it within 2 hours.

■ If you're eating later, divide hot food into shallow containers, cover them loosely, and refrigerate immediately.

■ Reheat thoroughly to a temperature of 165°F or until hot and steaming. In the microwave oven, cover food and rotate so that it heats evenly. Let the food stand for 2 minutes before eating for more thorough heating.

■ Keep cold food cold. Refrigerate it immediately.

■ Perishable food should not be at room temperature longer than 2 hours.

■ "If in doubt, throw it out."

About the Recipes

The recipes in this book were carefully chosen to help you make the most of your precious resources: health, wealth, and time. They have passed the taste and convenience tests of busy families and professionals who want to eat healthfully without squandering their money or their minutes. Our recipes reflect the money-saving principles described in the pages of this book, including the concepts of planned-overs and batch cooking.

The preparation time is given for each recipe. This is the actual hands-on time it takes to prepare the ingredients for the recipe. Marinating time, chilling time, and cooking time are not included. All of the recipes have been designed to improve your kitchen efficiency.

You may notice that the recipes are arranged a bit differently from the usual cookbook categories. They have been grouped according to their place on the Diabetes Food Pyramid from *The First Step in Diabetes Meal Planning*. You can easily refer back to "The Penny-Pincher's Food Pyramid" (chapter 4) for hints on choosing the most economical ingredients from each part of the pyramid. Notice that some of the recipes can easily fit in a different section. For example, some dessert recipes from "Fats, Sweets, and Alcohol" would be just as appropriate for "Fruits." This is another example of the versatility you can enjoy when planning your diabetes meals!

Although the recipes were designed to meet the guidelines from the 1994 "Nutrition Recommendations for People with Diabetes," you will note that several of the recipes that serve as one-dish meals have seemingly high sodium contents. Keep in mind that in these recipes one food will be serving as the majority of your meal. Consider how these recipes fit into your diabetes meal plan, particularly if you are restricting your sodium.

The cost per serving and prices noted in the text and recipes were calculated based on local supermarket prices in summer 1998. These prices may vary based on the marketplace, the season of the year, and the area of the country.

Nutrition analysis of recipes was performed using Nutritionist IV for Windows, Diet Analysis Module, Version 4.1 (First DataBank, San Bruno, CA). Food exchange information is based on the *1996 Exchange Lists for Meal Planning* (The American Dietetic Association and the American Diabetes Association).

Grains, Beans, and Starchy Vegetables

Fiery Pinto Beans

Cost per Serving

The cumin in this dish is used like a firefighter uses a hose—to cool down the heat! If you have any frozen leftover ham, just pull it out of the freezer for this recipe.

1 lb dried pinto beans

15 cups water, divided

1 cup chopped lean ham (approximately 5 oz)

1 large onion, chopped

1 4.5-oz can chopped green chilies

1 Tbsp ground cumin

1 Tbsp chili powder

1 tsp salt

1/4 tsp ground black pepper

Exchanges

1 Starch

1 Very Lean Meat

Calories 101

Calories from Fat 9

Total Fat 1 g

Saturated Fat <1 g

Cholesterol 6 mg

Sodium 367 mg

Carbohydrate 16 g

Dietary Fiber 6 g

Sugars <1 g

Protein 7 g

1. Sort and wash beans, then place them in a 1-gallon stockpot. Add 10 cups of water, the ham, and the onion. Cover and bring to a boil over high heat.

2. Reduce heat until beans are at a simmer (a gentle boil), and simmer covered for 2 hours, stirring beans occasionally. Add remaining water, chilies, cumin, chili powder, salt, and pepper; then stir to combine.

3. Continue cooking an additional 30 minutes or until beans are tender—again stirring periodically. If a thicker "soup" is desired, mash some of the beans with a spoon during this last half hour of cooking.

Simple Red Beans and Rice

Preparation Time:
15 minutes

Servings: 5

Serving Size:
1 cup beans,
1 cup rice

Cost per Serving

To remove the skin from fresh tomatoes, drop tomatoes in boiling water and leave them for 30 seconds. Remove with tongs and place gently in a pan of ice-cold water for 2 minutes. Tomato skins will easily peel off using your fingers.

Cooking spray

1 medium onion, chopped

1/2 medium green pepper, chopped

1 tsp minced garlic

1 Tbsp chili powder

1 tsp ground cumin

2 15.5-oz cans red beans, drained and rinsed

2 large fresh tomatoes, peeled and chopped

1/2 cup mild picanté sauce

5 cups hot, cooked brown rice

1. Coat a large nonstick skillet with cooking spray and warm over low-medium heat. Add onion, green pepper, and garlic and cook, stirring frequently, until onion is tender and translucent—about 5 minutes.

2. Add chili powder, cumin, beans, tomatoes, and picanté sauce. Cover and cook over low heat for 20 minutes.

3. Spoon 1 cup bean mixture over 1 cup rice to serve.

Exchanges

5 Starch

1 Vegetable

Calories 415

Calories from Fat
27

Total Fat 3 g

Saturated Fat <1 g

Cholesterol 0 mg

Sodium 558 mg

Carbohydrate 82 g

Dietary Fiber 13 g

Sugars 7 g

Protein 15 g

$0.18

Cost per Serving

Exchanges

2 Starch

1 Very Lean Meat

Calories 199

Calories from Fat
27

Total Fat 3 g

Saturated Fat 1 g

Cholesterol 19 mg

Sodium 615 mg

Carbohydrate 25 g

Dietary Fiber 6 g

Sugars 4 g

Protein 18 g

Sunday Afternoon
Split Pea Soup

A splendid soup to make on a lazy Sunday afternoon—let the soup simmer on the stove while you rest on the couch, then sit down to a filling meal of soup and Gran's Country-Style Corn Bread (p. 74). Try this after the holidays, using the holiday ham bone.

12 cups water, divided

1 medium onion, finely diced

2 cups chopped lean ham (about 10 oz) OR
    1 medium ham bone with fat removed

1 16-oz package dried split peas

1/2 tsp salt

1/4 tsp ground black pepper

1. Place 10 cups water, onion, and ham in a 1-gallon stockpot over high heat and bring to a boil. If ham bone is used, boil the bone in 10 cups water with onion for 30 minutes. Remove bone and gristle from pot and scrape remaining ham off bone. Slice meat into bite-sized pieces and return to the pot.

2. Meanwhile, place dried split peas in a colander and rinse under cool running water—remove any debris. Add peas to liquid and return to a boil.

3. Reduce heat until peas are at a simmer (a gentle boil), cover, and simmer for 1 1/2 hours, stirring periodically. Add remaining 2 cups water as needed during this cooking time.

4. Stir in salt and pepper and simmer over low heat for an additional 15 minutes—soup should be thick.

Beth's Black-Eyed Peas

Preparation Time:
15 minutes

Servings: 6

Serving Size:
1 cup

Serve as a side dish packed with fiber or over steaming rice for a filling main dish.

1 16-oz package dry black-eyed peas

8 cups cold water

6 cups warm water

2 cubes reduced-sodium beef bouillon

1 medium onion, finely diced

1/4 tsp salt

Cost per Serving

1. Rinse and sort peas. In a large pot, bring cold water and peas to a boil over high heat; boil for 2 minutes. Remove from heat, cover, and allow to soak for 1 hour. Drain off water and rinse peas.
2. Place soaked peas, warm water, bouillon cubes, and onion in a large pot. Bring to a boil over high heat. Reduce heat to low. Cook 45 minutes to 1 hour or until peas are tender, adding more warm water if necessary; stir periodically. Peas should be covered with a thick sauce.
3. Add salt, stir gently, and serve.

Exchanges

2 1/2 Starch

1 Very Lean Meat

Calories 221

Calories from Fat 9

Total Fat 1 g

Saturated Fat <1 g

Cholesterol 0 mg

Sodium 109 mg

Carbohydrate 39 g

Dietary Fiber 12 g

Sugars 6 g

Protein 14 g

Cost per Serving

Exchanges

1 1/2 Starch

Calories 138

Calories from Fat
18

Total Fat 2 g

Saturated Fat 1 g

Cholesterol 25 mg

Sodium 412 mg

Carbohydrate 25 g

Dietary Fiber <1 g

Sugars 2 g

Protein 5 g

Gran's Country-Style Corn Bread

For an extra special crunchy crust, try baking corn bread in an 8-inch iron skillet that has been heated in a 450°F oven then coated generously with cooking spray. Turn bread out of pan as soon as it's baked.

1 3/4 cups self-rising white cornmeal mix

1/4 cup all-purpose flour

1 egg

2 tsp corn oil

1 1/2 cups low-fat buttermilk

1. Preheat oven to 450°F. Place all ingredients in large mixing bowl and stir to combine.
2. Pour into 8 × 8-inch baking pan coated generously with cooking spray, and bake for 20 to 25 minutes or until corn bread is golden brown.
3. Slice into 9 equal squares.

Quick Garlic Buns

Preparation Time:
5 minutes

Servings: 6

Serving Size:
1/2 bun

Here's an imaginative and yummy way to use extra hamburger or hot dog buns, even if they are slightly stale!

3 hamburger or hot dog buns
6 tsp reduced-calorie tub margarine
1/4 tsp garlic salt

1. Preheat broiler. Open buns and lay on a baking sheet with the crust side down.
2. In a small bowl, combine margarine and garlic salt. Spread each bun half with 1 tsp of the margarine and garlic salt mixture.
3. Place in oven 5 inches from broiler, and broil with door slightly cracked until margarine is melted and buns are lightly toasted, about 3 minutes.

Cost per Serving

Exchanges

1 Starch

1/2 Fat

Calories 92

Calories from Fat 36

Total Fat 4 g

Saturated Fat <1 g

Cholesterol 0 mg

Sodium 144 mg

Carbohydrate 12 g

Dietary Fiber 0 g

Sugars 0 g

Protein 2 g

$0.03

Cost per Serving

Crunchy Croutons

Here's an economical way to use stale bread! These are tasty sprinkled on a green salad or a steaming bowl of soup.

1/4 tsp garlic salt

1/8 tsp onion powder

2 Tbsp reduced-calorie tub margarine, melted

4 slices white bread

1. Preheat oven to 400°F.
2. Stir garlic salt and onion powder into melted margarine. Using a pastry brush, coat both sides of each slice of bread with the margarine mixture, then lay bread on baking sheet. Cut bread into 1-inch cubes (16 per slice) and separate the cubes on the baking sheet.
3. Bake for 5 minutes, stir, then continue to bake until golden and crispy, about 4 minutes.

Exchanges

1/2 Starch

Calories 46

Calories from Fat 18

Total Fat 2 g

Saturated Fat <1 g

Cholesterol 0 mg

Sodium 161 mg

Carbohydrate 6 g

Dietary Fiber <1 g

Sugars <1 g

Protein 1 g

Banana-Oatmeal Muffins

Preparation Time:
25 minutes

Servings: 12

Serving Size:
1 muffin

If you're making these muffins for breakfast, combine the dry ingredients the night before to save time in the morning.

$0.06

Cost per Serving

1 cup old-fashioned rolled oats

3/4 cup fat-free (skim) milk

1 cup all-purpose flour

1/3 cup sugar

1 Tbsp baking powder

1/4 tsp salt

1/4 tsp cinnamon

1 egg, well beaten

3 Tbsp corn oil

1 ripe banana, mashed

Cooking spray

1. Preheat oven to 425°F. In a large mixing bowl, stir together oats and milk, then let stand 15 minutes.
2. In a separate bowl, sift together flour, sugar, baking powder, salt, and cinnamon. In a third bowl, combine egg, oil, and banana.
3. Add banana mixture to oat mixture. Stir in dry ingredients.
4. Line muffin pan with 12 paper baking cups, and coat with cooking spray. Spoon batter into baking cups, filling 3/4 full. Bake for 15 minutes or until muffins are golden and spring back when touched. Cool on rack.

Exchanges

1 Starch

1/2 Fruit

1/2 Fat

Calories 132

Calories from Fat 36

Total Fat 4 g

Saturated Fat 1 g

Cholesterol 18 mg

Sodium 252 mg

Carbohydrate 21 g

Dietary Fiber 1 g

Sugars 7 g

Protein 3 g

**Preparation Time:
25 minutes**

Servings: 16

**Serving Size:
1 muffin**

$0.14

Cost per Serving

Exchanges

1 Starch

1 Fruit

Calories 142

Calories from Fat
18

Total Fat 2 g

Saturated Fat <1 g

Cholesterol 1 mg

Sodium 188 mg

Carbohydrate 28 g

Dietary Fiber 1 g

Sugars 13 g

Protein 3 g

Orange Breakfast Muffins

*This mildly sweet muffin provides a change
from the usual cereal and milk. Serve with a
steaming cup of coffee or tea.*

1 orange

1 cup raisins

2 cups all-purpose flour

1 tsp baking soda

1/4 tsp salt

1/2 cup sugar

12 packets NutraSweet artificial sweetener

1/4 tsp ground cinnamon

1 cup low-fat buttermilk

6 Tbsp reduced-calorie stick margarine, melted

4 egg whites

Cooking spray

1/2 Tbsp sugar

1. Preheat oven to 400°F. Cut orange in half and
   squeeze juice out of each half; set juice aside.
   Remove pulp from orange rind and discard.
   Using a knife, scrape or cut out white stringy
   part of rind and discard. Place remaining orange
   rind and raisins in food processor (or use hand
   chopper) and pulse until rind and raisins are
   finely chopped.

2. Combine orange-raisin mixture, flour, baking
   soda, salt, sugar, NutraSweet, and cinnamon in
   a large mixing bowl. Make a well in the center
   of these dry ingredients.

3. In a separate bowl, combine buttermilk, margarine, and egg whites; mix well. Add wet ingredients to dry ingredients and stir until just moistened (batter will be lumpy).

4. Line muffin pan with 16 paper baking cups, then coat with cooking spray. Spoon batter into muffin cups, filling each cup 3/4 full. Bake for 13–15 minutes or until muffins are golden and spring back when touched. Turn out of pans to cool.

5. Brush muffins with reserved fresh orange juice (you probably won't use all of the juice), and sprinkle with the remaining 1/2 Tbsp sugar.

Golden Applesauce Muffins

$0.08

Cost per Serving

Applesauce lends a sweet flavor and replaces oil in these moist muffins.

1 1/4 cups all-purpose flour

1/2 tsp baking powder

1/2 tsp baking soda

1/8 tsp salt

1/3 cup sugar

2 cups bran flake cereal, crushed

1 1/4 cups fat-free (skim) milk

1 egg, beaten

1/3 cup unsweetened applesauce

Cooking spray

Exchanges

1 Starch

1 Fruit

Calories 141

Calories from Fat 9

Total Fat 1 g

Saturated Fat <1 g

Cholesterol 18 mg

Sodium 222 mg

Carbohydrate 29 g

Dietary Fiber 3 g

Sugars 9 g

Protein 4 g

1. Preheat oven to 400°F. In a mixing bowl, combine flour, baking powder, baking soda, salt, and sugar.

2. In a separate large mixing bowl, combine bran flakes and milk, then let stand until cereal is softened, about 2 minutes.

3. Stir in egg and applesauce, mixing well. Add dry ingredients and stir just until combined.

4. Line muffin tin with 12 paper baking cups, and coat with cooking spray. Spoon batter into baking cups, filling 3/4 full. Bake for 16 to 20 minutes, until muffins are golden and spring back when touched. Cool on rack.

Cinnamon French Toast

Preparation Time:
5 minutes

Servings: 4

Serving Size:
2 slices

This is a super way to use day-old or slightly stale bread. Try it with Wild Berry Syrup, p. 182!

1 egg + 2 egg whites

1/2 cup fat-free (skim) milk

1/4 tsp vanilla extract

1/8 tsp cinnamon

8 slices bread

Butter-flavored cooking spray

1. In a shallow dish, whisk together egg and egg whites, milk, vanilla, and cinnamon. Dip each slice of bread quickly in egg mixture to coat one side, flip over with fork and quickly coat other side.

2. Place in large nonstick skillet coated generously with cooking spray and warmed over medium heat. Cook until golden, turn over, and continue cooking until other side is golden. If cooking French toast in 2 batches, re-coat skillet with cooking spray between batches.

Cost per Serving

Exchanges

2 Starch

Calories 167

Calories from Fat 27

Total Fat 3 g

Saturated Fat 1 g

Cholesterol 54 mg

Sodium 302 mg

Carbohydrate 27 g

Dietary Fiber 1 g

Sugars 3 g

Protein 8 g

Preparation Time:
25 minutes

Servings: 5

Serving Size:
1 cup

$0.35

Cost per Serving

Exchanges

4 Carbohydrate

1 Fat

Calories 327

Calories from Fat
63

Total Fat 7 g

Saturated Fat 2 g

Cholesterol 44 mg

Sodium 577 mg

Carbohydrate 56 g

Dietary Fiber 2 g

Sugars 14 g

Protein 10 g

Spiced Raisin Bread Pudding

This is a simple way to transform day-old bread into a marvelous dessert. If the bread is not very dry, bake it in the oven at 350°F for 5 min to dry it out.

2 cups fat-free (skim) milk

4 Tbsp reduced-calorie stick margarine

6 cups cubed, dry day-old French bread
(approximately 1/2 lb)

1 egg + 2 egg whites

1/8 tsp ground cloves

1 1/2 tsp cinnamon

1/4 tsp salt

1 tsp vanilla extract

1/3 cup packed light brown sugar

6 packets NutraSweet artificial sweetener

1/2 cup raisins

Cooking spray

1. Preheat oven to 350°F. Warm milk and margarine in very large (about 5-quart) saucepan over medium heat until margarine is melted—do not boil. Remove from heat, stir in bread, and cool 10 minutes.

2. Meanwhile, combine egg and egg whites in a bowl and whisk until foamy. Mix in cloves, cinnamon, salt, vanilla extract, brown sugar, and sweetener. Add to cooled milk/bread and stir to combine.

3. Mix in raisins, and spoon pudding into 2-quart casserole dish coated with cooking spray. Bake for 30 minutes or until pudding is set and a toothpick inserted into the center of the pudding comes out clean.

Tempting Tomato and Macaroni Medley

Preparation Time:
10 minutes

Servings: 7

Serving Size:
1 cup

If fresh tomatoes are not in season, you can substitute 2 14.5-oz cans diced tomatoes, drained.

Cost per Serving

1 3/4 cups uncooked elbow macaroni OR 1 7-oz package

4 cups peeled, diced tomatoes

1 Tbsp + 1 tsp corn oil

1/4 tsp ground black pepper

1/8 tsp salt

1/8 tsp garlic powder

1. In a large pan, cook macaroni according to package directions, omitting salt if called for. Drain macaroni, return to pan, and add remaining ingredients.
2. Simmer uncovered over low-medium heat for 20 minutes or until tomatoes have cooked down—stir gently to prevent sticking.

Exchanges

1 Starch

1 1/2 Vegetable

Calories 135

Calories from Fat 27

Total Fat 3 g

Saturated Fat <1 g

Cholesterol 0 mg

Sodium 51 mg

Carbohydrate 23 g

Dietary Fiber 1 g

Sugars 3 g

Protein 4 g

**Preparation Time:
15 minutes**

Servings: 8

**Serving Size:
1 ear**

$0.29

Cost per Serving

Exchanges

1 Starch

Calories 87

Calories from Fat
27

Total Fat 3 g

Saturated Fat <1 g

Cholesterol 0 mg

Sodium 211 mg

Carbohydrate 12 g

Dietary Fiber 1 g

Sugars 2 g

Protein 3 g

Cheesy Corn on the Cob

One bite and you'll fall in love with corn.

8 ears corn, husks and silks removed
3 Tbsp reduced-calorie stick margarine, melted
1/4 tsp garlic salt
4 slices fat-free American cheese

1. Fill a 1-gallon pot half full with water and bring
   to a boil over high heat. Add corn and boil for
   7 minutes or until kernels are tender. Drain
   corn.

2. In a small bowl, combine melted margarine and
   garlic salt. Using a pastry brush, coat corn with
   margarine mixture.

3. Place in serving dish and lay 1/2 slice of cheese
   over each ear of corn. Allow to stand for
   5 minutes before serving so that cheese melts.

Rice Royale

Preparation Time:
5 minutes

Servings: 8

Serving Size:
1/2 cup

To make canned beef bouillon less fattening, chill bouillon in the refrigerator for at least 1 hour, then skim off the fat that rises to the top.

$0.22

Cost per Serving

3 Tbsp reduced-calorie stick margarine

1 cup uncooked long-grain white rice

1 7-oz can mushroom stems and pieces, drained

1/2 cup finely chopped onion

1 14.5-oz can reduced-sodium beef broth, chilled and fat removed

1/8 tsp ground black pepper

1 Tbsp chopped fresh parsley

1. Melt margarine in a large nonstick skillet over medium-high heat. Add uncooked rice, mushrooms, and onion. Cook, stirring constantly, until rice is golden (about 5 minutes).
2. Stir in beef broth and black pepper. Bring to a boil. Reduce heat to low, cover, and cook until rice is tender and liquid is absorbed (about 15 to 20 minutes)—stir periodically.
3. Fluff rice with a fork, sprinkle with parsley, and serve.

Exchanges

1 1/2 Starch

Calories 114

Calories from Fat 18

Total Fat 2 g

Saturated Fat <1 g

Cholesterol 0 mg

Sodium 171 mg

Carbohydrate 21 g

Dietary Fiber 1 g

Sugars 1 g

Protein 3 g

Oven-Baked Sweet Potatoes with Maple Cream

To save time, try microwaving the potatoes rather than oven-baking them. The maple cream is also tasty drizzled over cut-up fresh fruit.

4 medium sweet potatoes (approximately 1 1/2 lb total, or 6 oz each)

1/4 cup fat-free sour cream

1 Tbsp maple syrup

1/8 tsp vanilla extract

1/4 tsp cinnamon

1. Preheat oven to 400°F. Wash and dry potatoes. Pierce each 5 times with a fork and place on a baking sheet. Bake at 400°F for 45 to 60 minutes or until tender when pierced with a fork.

2. In a small bowl, whisk together sour cream, syrup, and vanilla extract.

3. Split each potato lengthwise, taking care not to cut all the way through. Spoon 1 Tbsp maple cream over each split potato, and sprinkle with cinnamon.

Exchanges

3 1/2 Starch

Calories 257

Calories from Fat 9

Total Fat 1 g

Saturated Fat <1 g

Cholesterol 0 mg

Sodium 80 mg

Carbohydrate 57 g

Dietary Fiber 1 g

Sugars 13 g

Protein 5 g

Sassy Sweet Potato Chips

Preparation Time:
20 minutes

Servings: 5

Serving Size:
1 cup

Chili powder and cumin complement the sweetness of these chips.

4 medium sweet potatoes (approximately 1 1/2 lb total, or 6 oz each)

4 tsp corn oil

1/4 tsp chili powder

1/4 tsp ground cumin

1/8 tsp ground black pepper

1/4 tsp salt

Cooking spray

Cost per Serving

1. Preheat oven to 375°F. Peel sweet potatoes, slice into 1/8-inch thick slices, then place in a bowl or baking pan.
2. Combine oil and seasonings in a small bowl. Drizzle over potatoes, then toss to coat potato slices well.
3. Place potato slices in a single layer on a baking pan coated with cooking spray. Bake for 10 minutes. Turn chips over and bake an additional 30 minutes, turning chips every 10 minutes. To prevent heat loss, remove pan from oven and close oven door when turning chips. (Watch closely during last 5 minutes of baking to prevent burning—you may need to remove smaller chips early.)
4. Transfer chips to wire rack to cool.

Exchanges

3 Starch

1/2 Fat

Calories 248

Calories from Fat 36

Total Fat 4 g

Saturated Fat 1 g

Cholesterol 0 mg

Sodium 175 mg

Carbohydrate 50 g

Dietary Fiber 1 g

Sugars 9 g

Protein 3 g

Preparation Time:
15 minutes

Servings: 6

Serving Size:
1 whole potato,
or 4–6 crisps

$0.09

Cost per Serving

Exchanges

1 1/2 Starch

1/2 Fat

Calories 147

Calories from Fat
27

Total Fat 3 g

Saturated Fat 1 g

Cholesterol 0 mg

Sodium 134 mg

Carbohydrate 27 g

Dietary Fiber 2 g

Sugars 1 g

Protein 3 g

Seasoned Potato Skin Crisps

Stir chopped chives into fat-free sour cream for a terrific topper!

6 medium baking potatoes (approximately 2 lb total)

3 Tbsp reduced-calorie stick margarine

1/4 tsp seasoned salt

1/8 tsp garlic powder

Paprika

1. Preheat oven to 400°F. Wrap clean potatoes in foil and bake for 1 hour and 15 minutes or until tender when pierced with a fork. Unwrap potatoes, cut in half lengthwise, and cool 10 minutes to prevent a burn and allow easier slicing.

2. Scoop out potato pulp (a melon-ball scoop works well), leaving a 1/4-inch layer of pulp on skin. Set pulp aside (can use to make mashed potatoes). Gently cut potato skins lengthwise into 1-inch strips (4–6 strips per potato).

3. In a small saucepan, melt margarine. Stir in seasoned salt and garlic powder. Using a pastry brush, coat potato skins with seasoned margarine.

4. Place skins on two baking sheets and bake for 25 minutes or until crisp. Sprinkle with paprika before serving.

Roasted Barbecue Potatoes

Preparation Time:
25 minutes

Servings: 6

Serving Size:
1 potato, or
1/6 recipe

Cost per Serving

These potatoes make a nice complement to sizzling hamburgers just off the grill.

6 medium baking potatoes, unpeeled

Cooking spray

1 large onion, thinly sliced and separated into rings

3 Tbsp all-purpose flour

2 1/4 cups cold water

3/4 cup barbecue sauce

1 Tbsp white vinegar

1/2 tsp salt

1/8 tsp ground black pepper

1. Preheat oven to 375°F. Thinly slice (1/8 inch thick) potatoes and layer in a 9 × 13-inch pan coated with cooking spray. Top potatoes with onion rings and set aside.

2. In a large bowl, whisk together flour and water. Whisk in barbecue sauce, vinegar, salt, and pepper. Pour over potatoes, cover with foil, and bake for 1 hour—stir every 30 minutes.

3. Remove foil after 1 hour baking time, return potatoes to oven, and continue baking an additional 45 minutes or until potatoes are tender when pierced with a fork.

Exchanges

4 Starch

Calories 297

Calories from Fat 5

Total Fat <1 g

Saturated Fat <1 g

Cholesterol 0 mg

Sodium 651 mg

Carbohydrate 67 g

Dietary Fiber 6 g

Sugars 12 g

Protein 6 g

Servings: 4

**Serving Size:
1 potato, or
1/4 recipe**

$0.15

Cost per Serving

Exchanges

2 1/2 Starch

Calories 198

Calories from Fat
18

Total Fat 2 g

Saturated Fat <1 g

Cholesterol 0 mg

Sodium 336 mg

Carbohydrate 41 g

Dietary Fiber 4 g

Sugars 3 g

Protein 4 g

Skillet Potatoes

*This versatile dish is a country-style favorite.
Serve it up in your most colorful bowl as a side
for almost any breakfast, lunch, or supper!*

4 medium potatoes, unpeeled, thinly sliced

Cooking spray

1 small onion, sliced and separated into rings

1 1/2 cups water

1 Tbsp reduced-calorie margarine

1/2 tsp salt

1/8 tsp ground black pepper

1/4 tsp garlic powder

1. Spread potatoes over bottom of a large nonstick
   skillet coated with cooking spray. Cover with
   rings of onion. Pour water over potatoes and
   onions, then dot with margarine. Cover skillet
   and cook over medium-high heat for
   15 minutes or until potatoes are tender.

2. Remove lid and continue cooking, allowing
   liquid to evaporate—do not stir. Sprinkle
   potatoes/onions evenly with salt, pepper, and
   garlic powder.

3. When potatoes cook dry, turn them over gently
   with a spatula (some slices may break).
   Continue cooking an additional 5 minutes.
   Potatoes will be tender with some slices a light
   golden brown.

Carrots, Onions, and Potatoes

This vegetable medley makes a savory accompaniment to the Dijon-Crusted Beef Roast, p. 152—both recipes bake at the same temperature.

3 carrots, peeled and sliced into bite-sized chunks

1 large onion, sliced and separated into rings

3 large potatoes, peeled and cut into bite-sized chunks

1 Tbsp reduced-calorie margarine

1/4 tsp salt

1/4 tsp ground black pepper

1/8 tsp garlic powder

1/2 cup fat-free, reduced-sodium chicken broth

1. Preheat oven to 325°F. Place carrots, onion, potatoes, and margarine on a large piece of wide foil, and then place foil with vegetables in a 9 × 13-inch baking pan.

2. Sprinkle vegetables evenly with salt, pepper, and garlic powder. Drizzle chicken broth over top. Seal foil to make a packet. Bake for 1 1/2 hours or until vegetables are tender.

3. Use caution when opening the packet to avoid being burned by hot steam! Stir vegetables to coat, then serve.

Preparation Time:
15 minutes

Servings: 6

Serving Size:
1/6 recipe

$0.20

Cost per Serving

Exchanges

1 Starch

1 Vegetable

Calories 117

Calories from Fat 9

Total Fat 1 g

Saturated Fat <1 g

Cholesterol 0 mg

Sodium 148 mg

Carbohydrate 24 g

Dietary Fiber 1 g

Sugars 3 g

Protein 3 g

Preparation Time:
5 minutes

Servings: 4

Serving Size:
1/2 cup

Cost per Serving

Exchanges

1 Starch

1 Very Lean Meat

1/2 Fat

Calories 144

Calories from Fat
36

Total Fat 4 g

Saturated Fat 1 g

Cholesterol 1 mg

Sodium 245 mg

Carbohydrate 19 g

Dietary Fiber <1 g

Sugars 4 g

Protein 8 g

Creamy Peas with Mushrooms

Here's another complementary side dish for Dijon-Crusted Beef Roast, p. 152.

2 Tbsp reduced-calorie stick margarine

1/3 cup chopped onion

1 Tbsp all-purpose flour

1/4 tsp salt

Dash ground black pepper

1 cup fat-free (skim) milk

1 cup sliced fresh mushrooms

1 14.5-oz can peas, drained and rinsed

1. In a nonstick skillet, melt margarine over medium heat. Add onion and sauté until tender. Stir in flour, salt, and pepper—will be pasty.

2. Add milk and mix with a wire whisk until thickened and bubbly, about 3 minutes. Add mushrooms then cook and stir for 2 minutes more.

3. Reduce heat to medium-low, add peas, and cook 5 additional minutes, stirring periodically.

Vegetables

Crunchy Oriental Coleslaw

Preparation Time:
20 minutes

Servings: 8

Serving Size:
1 cup

Cost per Serving

Exchanges

2 Vegetable

3 Fat

Calories 186

Calories from Fat
126

Total Fat 14 g

Saturated Fat 2 g

Cholesterol 0 mg

Sodium 422 mg

Carbohydrate 12 g

Dietary Fiber 2 g

Sugars 3 g

Protein 3 g

Try this coleslaw at your next picnic or potluck!

Dressing
1/3 cup corn oil

3 Tbsp white vinegar

2 tsp sugar

1/2 tsp salt

1/2 tsp ground black pepper

Seasoning packet from Oriental Ramen noodles

Salad
1 lb green cabbage, shredded

6 green onions, chopped

1 3.5-oz package Oriental Ramen noodles, crumbled

1/3 cup dry roasted sunflower seeds

1. In a small jar, combine dressing ingredients. Place lid tightly on jar and shake to combine. Dressing flavor is enhanced if made ahead and chilled in the refrigerator for about 1 hour before tossing with salad.

2. In a large bowl, combine salad ingredients. Toss dressing with salad and serve immediately to maintain crunchiness.

Marinated Confetti Vegetable Salad

Preparation Time:
15 minutes

Servings: 6

Serving Size:
1/2 cup

The marinade lends a mild tanginess to this colorful and crunchy salad that incorporates tomatoes and cucumbers fresh from the garden.

Cost per Serving

Marinade

3 Tbsp white wine vinegar

1 1/2 tsp corn oil

1 tsp Dijon mustard

1 tsp (or 1 clove) minced garlic

1/4 tsp salt

1/8 tsp ground black pepper

Salad

1 15.25-oz can white corn, drained and rinsed

1 cup diced tomato

1 cup peeled, diced cucumber

1. Place marinade ingredients in a jar, cover tightly with lid, and shake to blend.
2. Combine corn, tomato, and cucumber in serving dish. Pour marinade over vegetables and toss to coat.
3. Cover and refrigerate for 1 hour to allow flavors to blend—stir twice while chilling.

Exchanges

1/2 Starch

1 Vegetable

1/2 Fat

Calories 78

Calories from Fat
  18

Total Fat 2 g

Saturated Fat <1 g

Cholesterol 0 mg

Sodium 303 mg

Carbohydrate 13 g

Dietary Fiber 1 g

Sugars 3 g

Protein 2 g

$0.63

Cost per Serving

Tomato Salad Surprise

The surprise ingredient in this salad is French bread cubes. Day-old French bread works best. If the bread is not very dry, bake it in the oven at 350°F for 5 minutes before cubing.

5 large, juicy, cold, ripe tomatoes, peeled (approximately 3 lb)

2 Tbsp corn oil

1 Tbsp red wine vinegar

2 tsp (or 2 cloves) minced garlic

1/2 tsp salt

3 cups French bread cubes, crust removed (use approximately 2/3 of 1-lb loaf)

1 Tbsp chopped fresh parsley

Exchanges

2 Starch

1 Vegetable

1 1/2 Fat

Calories 244

Calories from Fat 72

Total Fat 8 g

Saturated Fat 1 g

Cholesterol 0 mg

Sodium 587 mg

Carbohydrate 37 g

Dietary Fiber 3 g

Sugars 3 g

Protein 6 g

1. Dice two tomatoes into bite-sized pieces and place in serving dish. Put remaining three tomatoes in food processor and pulse until tomatoes are a coarse puree (you may also mash the tomatoes by hand).

2. Add puree, oil, vinegar, garlic, and salt to diced tomatoes; stir well. Toss bread cubes into tomato mixture, sprinkle with parsley, and serve immediately.

Cucumbers and Onions in Dill Dressing

Savor just a hint of dill in this creamy sweet 'n' sour salad!

2 large cucumbers, peeled and thinly sliced

1/2 medium onion, thinly sliced and separated into rings

Dressing

1/2 cup fat-free mayonnaise

1 Tbsp + 1 tsp white vinegar

1/4 tsp dill weed

1 packet NutraSweet artificial sweetener

1. Combine cucumbers and onion in a serving dish. In a separate bowl, whisk together mayonnaise, vinegar, dill weed, and sweetener.
2. Pour dressing over vegetables and toss to coat. Cover salad and chill for 30 minutes for best flavor.

Preparation Time: 15 minutes

Servings: 4

Serving Size: 1 cup

$0.54

Cost per Serving

Exchanges

2 Vegetable

Calories 45

Calories from Fat 5

Total Fat <1 g

Saturated Fat <1 g

Cholesterol 0 mg

Sodium 215 mg

Carbohydrate 9 g

Dietary Fiber 1 g

Sugars 5 g

Protein 1 g

Preparation Time:
10 minutes

Servings: 6

Serving Size:
1 cup

$0.68

Cost per Serving

Exchanges

1 Starch

2 Vegetable

1/2 Fat

Calories 162

Calories from Fat
18

Total Fat 2 g

Saturated Fat 1 g

Cholesterol 3 mg

Sodium 400 mg

Carbohydrate 26 g

Dietary Fiber 3 g

Sugars 3 g

Protein 10 g

Feisty French Onion Soup

This soup is just as flavorful reheated!

3 large onions, thinly sliced and separated into
  rings

5 1/2 cups OR 3 14.5-oz cans reduced-sodium
  beef broth, fat removed

1 Tbsp Worcestershire sauce

1/4 tsp salt

1/8 tsp ground black pepper

6 1-inch slices French bread, lightly toasted

1/3 cup shredded part-skim mozzarella cheese

1. In a 4- to 5-quart saucepan, sauté onion in
   1 cup beef broth over high heat until slightly
   tender (about 5 minutes)—stir periodically.

2. Add remaining broth, Worcestershire sauce,
   salt, and pepper. Simmer covered over medium
   heat for 20 minutes.

3. Place toasted bread on baking sheet and
   sprinkle with cheese. Broil 5 inches from heat
   source for 2 minutes or until cheese melts. Cut
   each piece of toast into 3 strips.

4. Pour soup into 6 bowls and top each with
   3 strips of cheese toast.

Favorite Vegetable Soup

Preparation Time:
25 minutes

Servings: 14

Serving Size:
1 cup

Cost per Serving

Vegetable soup is a great way to use leftover vegetables and even meat—replace each can of vegetable listed in the recipe with approximately 2 cups of that same vegetable from your leftovers. Also, you can replace ground chuck with 1/2 lb leftover shredded roast beef.

1/2 lb ground chuck
7 cups peeled, chopped fresh tomatoes OR
    2 28-oz cans diced tomatoes*
4 cups water
1 14.5-oz can cut green beans, drained and rinsed
1 15-oz can peas, drained and rinsed
1 15.25-oz can corn, drained and rinsed
2 carrots, peeled and chopped
3 potatoes, peeled and diced
1 medium onion, diced
1/4 cup dry rice
1/8 tsp ground black pepper
1/8 tsp red pepper flakes
1/2 tsp salt
1/2 tsp garlic powder

1. Place ground chuck in a 2-gallon stockpot and brown over medium heat. Remove meat and drain it well. Wipe drippings from pot.
2. Return meat to stockpot, then add tomatoes and water. Bring to simmer and cook, covered, until tomatoes are soft and a juicy broth is created, about 20 minutes.
3. Add remaining ingredients, cover, and continue cooking 60 additional minutes to allow flavors to blend.

*Note: Using canned tomatoes will increase the sodium content of this dish.

Exchanges

1 Starch

1 Vegetable

1 Very Lean Meat

Calories 155

Calories from Fat
  27

Total Fat 3 g

Saturated Fat 1 g

Cholesterol 17 mg

Sodium 185 mg

Carbohydrate 23 g

Dietary Fiber 2 g

Sugars 5 g

Protein 9 g

Garden Vegetable Scramble

Servings: 12

Serving Size:
1/2 cup

Cost per Serving

This makes a colorful side dish—or a meatless meal when served with a slice of Gran's Country-Style Corn Bread, p. 74!

3 cups shredded green cabbage

2 ears corn, cut from cob

2 medium zucchini, chopped

1 large onion, chopped

3 medium fresh banana peppers, seeded and chopped

3 large tomatoes, peeled and chopped

1/8 cup water

1 1/2 Tbsp corn oil

1/8 tsp red pepper flakes

1/2 tsp salt

1/8 tsp ground black pepper

Exchanges

2 Vegetable

1. Combine all ingredients in a large pan. Simmer, uncovered, over medium heat for 25 minutes, stirring periodically.

Calories 54

Calories from Fat 18

Total Fat 2 g

Saturated Fat <1 g

Cholesterol 0 mg

Sodium 105 mg

Carbohydrate 8 g

Dietary Fiber 2 g

Sugars 3 g

Protein 1 g

Tangy Carrot Coins

Preparation Time:
10 minutes

Servings: 4

Serving Size:
1/2 cup

The tartness of cider vinegar is a nice complement to the carrots' sweetness.

1 lb carrots, peeled and sliced into 1/8-inch-thick coins

1/2 cup water

1/3 cup cider vinegar

2 Tbsp reduced-calorie margarine

1/2 tsp dried crushed parsley

1/4 tsp salt

1/8 tsp ground black pepper

Paprika

Cost per Serving

1. Place carrot coins in a large saucepan, add water, and cover pan. Bring to a boil, reduce heat to medium, and simmer 10 minutes or until carrots are crisp-tender. Drain and place in serving dish.
2. In a small saucepan, combine vinegar, margarine, parsley, salt, and pepper; heat until margarine melts. Drizzle over cooked carrots. Sprinkle with paprika.

Exchanges

2 Vegetable

1/2 Fat

Calories 79

Calories from Fat 27

Total Fat 3 g

Saturated Fat 1 g

Cholesterol 0 mg

Sodium 269 mg

Carbohydrate 12 g

Dietary Fiber <1 g

Sugars 7 g

Protein 1 g

Cauliflower Sauté

Cost per Serving

Garlic's mellow taste is a remarkable complement to cauliflower in this recipe.

1 head cauliflower, cut into bite-sized florets

2 Tbsp reduced-calorie margarine

1 1/2 tsp corn oil

1 tsp (or 1 clove) minced garlic

1/4 tsp salt

1/8 tsp ground black pepper

Paprika

1. Place cauliflower florets in a steamer basket above 2 inches boiling water. Cover and steam about 4 to 5 minutes or until cauliflower is crisp-tender when pierced with a fork. Remove from steam and keep warm.

2. Melt margarine in a large nonstick skillet. Add oil and garlic; sauté garlic over medium heat for 2 minutes.

3. Add steamed cauliflower and toss to coat. Continue sautéing for 5 additional minutes, stirring periodically.

4. Sprinkle with salt and pepper and toss. Place in serving dish and sprinkle with paprika.

Exchanges

1 Vegetable

1/2 Fat

Calories 43

Calories from Fat 27

Total Fat 3 g

Saturated Fat <1 g

Cholesterol 0 mg

Sodium 147 mg

Carbohydrate 3 g

Dietary Fiber 1 g

Sugars 1 g

Protein 1 g

Grilled Onion Slices

Preparation Time:
5 minutes

Servings: 6

Serving Size:
2 slices

Use Vidalias or any sweet onion for the finest taste! For ease in grilling onions, use a grill basket or cover grill grate with foil, then cut slits in foil.

2 large onions, cut into 1/4-inch slices
   (approximately 6 slices per onion)
3 Tbsp reduced-calorie stick margarine, melted
1/4 tsp coarse ground black pepper
1/2 tsp garlic salt

1. Combine melted margarine, pepper, and garlic salt, mixing well. Brush both sides of onion slices (take care not to separate the rings) with margarine mixture.
2. Grill over hot coals 4 minutes per side, turning only once. Baste with remaining margarine throughout cooking. Onions slices will be slightly charred.

Cost per Serving

Exchanges

3 Vegetable (or
   1 Carbohydrate)

1/2 Fat

Calories 99

Calories from Fat
   27

Total Fat 3 g

Saturated Fat 1 g

Cholesterol 0 mg

Sodium 243 mg

Carbohydrate 16 g

Dietary Fiber 3 g

Sugars 3 g

Protein 2 g

Cost per Serving

Garlic-Parmesan Mushrooms

This easy appetizer is just bursting with flavor!

1 lb mushrooms, cleaned and stems removed

3 Tbsp reduced-calorie stick margarine, melted

1/4 tsp garlic salt

Cooking spray

1/8 cup grated Parmesan cheese

Paprika

1. Preheat broiler. Place cleaned mushrooms in a bowl. Combine margarine and garlic salt, then drizzle over mushrooms. Gently toss mushrooms to coat.

2. Spray a 9 × 13-inch baking sheet with sides (or a 9 × 13-inch pan) with cooking spray. Place mushrooms on baking sheet, stem-side up. Sprinkle with cheese then lightly with paprika.

3. Broil 5 inches from heat source (crack oven door) for 5 minutes or until cheese is slightly melted. Serve immediately.

Exchanges

1 Fat

Calories 52

Calories from Fat 36

Total Fat 4 g

Saturated Fat 1 g

Cholesterol 1 mg

Sodium 139 mg

Carbohydrate 2 g

Dietary Fiber 0 g

Sugars 1 g

Protein 2 g

Southern-Style Green Beans

Preparation Time: 15 minutes

Servings: 6

Serving Size: 1/2 cup

Beef bouillon and onions lend southern flavor without the fat that traditional bacon or ham hocks add.

Cost per Serving

1 lb fresh green beans

2 1/2 cups water

2 tsp corn oil

2 cubes reduced-sodium beef bouillon

1/4 cup finely diced onion

1/8 tsp salt

1. Remove strings from green beans, then break beans into bite-sized pieces. Wash beans and place in 2-quart pan. Add water, oil, bouillon cubes, and onion. Bring to a simmer.
2. Cover and cook for 30 minutes or until beans are tender when pierced with a fork; stir periodically. Add salt, stir, and continue cooking an additional 60 minutes—most of the liquid should evaporate, and the beans should be very tender.

Exchanges

1 Vegetable

1/2 Fat

Calories 38

Calories from Fat 18

Total Fat 2 g

Saturated Fat <1 g

Cholesterol 0 mg

Sodium 56 mg

Carbohydrate 4 g

Dietary Fiber 1 g

Sugars 1 g

Protein 1 g

Preparation Time:
5 minutes

Servings: 8

Serving Size:
1/2 cup

Cost per Serving

Exchanges

1 Vegetable

Calories 20

Calories from Fat 2

Total Fat <1 g

Saturated Fat <1 g

Cholesterol 0 mg

Sodium 88 mg

Carbohydrate 3 g

Dietary Fiber 2 g

Sugars 1 g

Protein 2 g

Broccoli Italiano

Italian dressing gives a nice zing to broccoli that's cooked just right—tender, but still a little crisp!

1 lb fresh (or thawed frozen) broccoli florets

1/4 cup fat-free Italian salad dressing

1. Place broccoli florets in steamer basket above 2 inches boiling water. Cover and steam 4 minutes or until broccoli is bright green and crisp-tender when pierced with a fork.

2. Remove from steam and place broccoli in serving dish. Drizzle with Italian dressing and toss to coat. Serve immediately.

Squash Medley

$0.51

Cost per Serving

Fresh squash should be heavy and firm, with a thin skin that can be punctured easily. If only hard-skinned squash is available, it should be peeled and seeded before cooking.

3 medium yellow summer squash, sliced 1/4 inch thick (approximately 1 3/4 lb)

3 medium zucchini squash, sliced 1/4 inch thick (approximately 1 1/2 lb)

1 medium onion, sliced 1/8 inch thick and separated into rings

6 cups water (just enough to cover squash)

2 Tbsp reduced-calorie margarine

1/4 tsp salt

1/8 tsp ground black pepper

1/8 tsp garlic powder

1. Combine all ingredients in a 4-quart saucepan.
2. Cook uncovered over medium-high heat for 30 minutes or until vegetables are tender—if desired, may continue cooking to allow extra liquid to evaporate.

Exchanges

2 Vegetable

1/2 Fat

Calories 70

Calories from Fat
  18

Total Fat 2 g

Saturated Fat <1 g

Cholesterol 0 mg

Sodium 123 mg

Carbohydrate 11 g

Dietary Fiber 3 g

Sugars 5 g

Protein 2 g

Tasty Cooked Greens

Preparation Time:
20 minutes

Servings: 6

Serving Size:
1 cup

Cost per Serving

Exchanges

3 Vegetable (or
   1 Carbohydrate)

1/2 Fat

Calories 114

Calories from Fat
   18

Total Fat 2 g

Saturated Fat <1 g

Cholesterol 0 mg

Sodium 243 mg

Carbohydrate 18 g

Dietary Fiber 2 g

Sugars 4 g

Protein 6 g

Use mustard, turnip, kale, or collard greens in this recipe.

2 lb fresh, tender greens
2 tsp corn oil
1/2 cup chopped onion
1 1/2 cups water
1 cube reduced-sodium chicken bouillon
1/4 tsp salt
1/8 tsp sugar
1 dash Tabasco sauce

1. Remove stems and any yellowed leaves from greens, then rinse greens well and drain.
2. Heat oil in a large pot over medium heat. Add onion and sauté until onion is tender.
3. Add greens, water, and bouillon to the pot. Cover and bring to a boil. Reduce heat to low and simmer for 30 minutes or until greens are tender, stirring occasionally.
4. Add salt, sugar, and Tabasco sauce. Toss well and simmer an additional 5 minutes.

Okra Jumble

Preparation Time:
25 minutes

Servings: 5

Serving Size:
1 cup

Cost per Serving

Green, white, red, and yellow—okra, onion, tomatoes, and corn lend a jumble of colors and flavors to this simple dish!

2 Tbsp reduced-calorie margarine

1 cup chopped onion

3 cups sliced tender okra (approximately 3/4 lb)

3 1/2 cups peeled, diced tomatoes OR 2 14.5-oz cans diced tomatoes*

2 cups fresh corn (approximately four 7-inch ears)

1/2 tsp salt

1/8 tsp ground black pepper

1 dash Tabasco sauce

1. Melt margarine in a large pan, add onion, and cook over medium heat until onion is tender, about 5 minutes.

2. Add okra and cook 5 more minutes, stirring periodically.

3. Mix in tomatoes, corn, salt, pepper, and Tabasco. Cover and simmer over low heat for 25 minutes or until corn and okra are tender; stir occasionally.

*Note: Using canned tomatoes will increase the sodium content of this dish.

Exchanges

1 Starch

1 Vegetable

1 Fat

Calories 143

Calories from Fat 27

Total Fat 3 g

Saturated Fat 1 g

Cholesterol 0 mg

Sodium 324 mg

Carbohydrate 25 g

Dietary Fiber 3 g

Sugars 7 g

Protein 4 g

Fruits

Strawberry Ribbon Supreme

Preparation Time:
15 minutes

Servings: 9

Serving Size:
1 square

$0.54

Cost per Serving

This colorful creation is delicious served as a salad or a dessert.

2 0.3-oz packages sugar-free strawberry gelatin

1 2/3 cups boiling water

1 10-oz package unsweetened frozen strawberries, sliced

2 bananas, sliced

1 15.25-oz can crushed pineapple in juice, drained well

4 oz reduced-fat cream cheese, softened

3 packets NutraSweet artificial sweetener

2 cups fat-free sour cream

Exchanges

1 Fruit

1/2 Fat-Free Milk

1 Very Lean Meat

Calories 138

Calories from Fat 18

Total Fat 2 g

Saturated Fat 1 g

Cholesterol 4 mg

Sodium 138 mg

Carbohydrate 20 g

Dietary Fiber 2 g

Sugars 13 g

Protein 10 g

1. In a large bowl, dissolve gelatin in boiling water. Add frozen strawberries and stir until berries are thawed. Add bananas; then place gelatin in refrigerator for 5 minutes or until gelatin is slightly thickened. Remove from refrigerator and stir in drained pineapple.

2. Spoon half of gelatin mixture into an 8 × 8-inch pan and refrigerate 10 minutes. Leave remaining gelatin out of refrigerator.

3. Meanwhile, place cream cheese and NutraSweet in a mixing bowl, and beat with an electric mixer until light and fluffy. Add sour cream and beat until mixture is smooth.

4. Remove gelatin from refrigerator and cover with cream cheese/sour cream mixture. Spoon remaining gelatin over and return to refrigerator. Chill until firm (about 30 minutes), then slice into 9 servings.

Fruit Fantasia

Preparation Time:
15 minutes

Servings: 12

Serving Size:
1/2 cup

Delight friends and family with this colorful salad or dessert! If chilling for more than 30 minutes, leave out the bananas, then toss them in just before serving.

2 bananas, sliced

2 cups sliced fresh strawberries

1 20-oz can pineapple tidbits in juice, drain and reserve juice

1 15-oz can sliced peaches in juice, drain and reserve juice

1 tsp sugar-free Tang drink mix

1 0.9-oz package sugar-free vanilla instant pudding mix

1. In a large serving dish, combine bananas, strawberries, pineapple, and peaches; set aside.

2. In a separate bowl, combine reserved pineapple juice, Tang mix, and pudding mix. Mix well using a wire whisk—it will be thick.

3. Spoon pudding mixture over fruit and toss gently to coat. May thin with reserved peach juice as desired. Chill 30 minutes before serving.

Cost per Serving

Exchanges

1 Fruit

Calories 69

Calories from Fat 5

Total Fat <1 g

Saturated Fat <1 g

Cholesterol 0 mg

Sodium 49 mg

Carbohydrate 15 g

Dietary Fiber 2 g

Sugars 10 g

Protein 1 g

$0.13

Cost per Serving

Cinnamon-Glazed Bananas

Cinnamon and orange juice complement the natural sweetness of bananas in this simple dessert.

3 small, firm, ripe bananas

2 Tbsp reduced-calorie margarine

2 Tbsp packed light brown sugar

3 Tbsp thawed unsweetened orange juice concentrate

1 tsp vanilla extract

1/4 tsp ground cinnamon

6 Tbsp frozen fat-free whipped topping

1. Peel bananas and cut in half lengthwise, then cut in half crosswise.

2. Melt margarine in a large nonstick skillet over medium heat. Add brown sugar, orange juice concentrate, vanilla extract, and cinnamon. Heat for 30 seconds while stirring constantly.

3. Add banana quarters and cook for 1 minute. Gently turn banana quarters and cook 1 additional minute.

4. Remove bananas to individual serving dishes, spoon sauce over, and top each serving with 1 Tbsp frozen whipped topping.

Exchanges

1 1/2 Fruit

1/2 Fat

Calories 116

Calories from Fat 27

Total Fat 3 g

Saturated Fat <1 g

Cholesterol <1 mg

Sodium 52 mg

Carbohydrate 23 g

Dietary Fiber 1 g

Sugars 13 g

Protein 1 g

Dessert Fruit Pizza

This dessert twist on pizza has a gelatin "crust" with fresh fruit toppings. It's a great way to use any fresh fruit you have on hand!

4 0.3-oz packages sugar-free raspberry gelatin

2 cups boiling water

Cooking spray

2 cups frozen "lite" whipped topping, thawed

1/2 cup sliced strawberries

1 banana, thinly sliced

1/2 cup green grapes, sliced lengthwise

2 2-inch graham cracker squares, crushed

Cost per Serving

1. In a large mixing bowl, combine gelatin and boiling water, stirring until gelatin is dissolved. Pour gelatin into a 12-inch pizza pan (with edges)* that has been coated with cooking spray.
2. Allow pan to sit on countertop about 1 hour, or until gelatin has thickened, to prevent spilling when moving pan to refrigerator. Place gently in refrigerator and chill until firm, about 1 hour.
3. After chilled, spread whipped topping on gelatin, leaving a 1-inch edge of gelatin showing. Top with strawberry, banana, and grape slices.
4. Sprinkle with crushed graham crackers, slice like a pizza, and serve. If serving will be delayed, wait to add banana slices and crushed graham crackers at serving time.

*A deep-dish pizza pan works best.

Exchanges

1/2 Fruit

1/2 Fat

Calories 58

Calories from Fat 18

Total Fat 2 g

Saturated Fat <1 g

Cholesterol <1 mg

Sodium 119 mg

Carbohydrate 8 g

Dietary Fiber 1 g

Sugars 5 g

Protein 2 g

$0.89

Cost per Serving

Exchanges

2 1/2 Fruit

Calories 173

Calories from Fat 9

Total Fat 1 g

Saturated Fat <1 g

Cholesterol 1 mg

Sodium 32 mg

Carbohydrate 39 g

Dietary Fiber 5 g

Sugars 19 g

Protein 2 g

Fresh Pears with Berries and "Cream"

Enjoy fresh, juicy pears nestled in a rich tasting "cream" created by combining vanilla yogurt, orange juice, and honey.

1 8-oz container sugar-free, fat-free vanilla yogurt

1 Tbsp unsweetened orange juice

1/4 cup honey

6 pears (approximately 3 1/4 lb)

1/2 cup fresh blueberries

1/2 cup fresh raspberries

Ground cinnamon

1. In a medium bowl, whisk together yogurt, orange juice, and honey; set aside.

2. Peel, core, and thinly slice each pear lengthwise. Arrange pear slices on 6 plates.

3. Spoon yogurt mixture over each pear, and sprinkle with both blueberries and raspberries. Sprinkle lightly with cinnamon and serve immediately.

Frozen Hawaiian Fruit Salad

This can also be served as a light dessert.

1 20-oz can crushed pineapple in juice

Water

18 oz frozen unsweetened pineapple-orange-banana juice concentrate, thawed

2 medium bananas, quartered lengthwise and diced into bite-sized chunks

1 15-oz can mandarin oranges, drained and rinsed, each slice cut in half

24 paper baking cups

Lettuce leaves, optional

1. Drain pineapple using a sieve, reserving juice in a 2-cup liquid measuring cup. Add water to reserved juice to make 1 1/2 cups liquid.
2. Pour liquid into a large mixing bowl. Add pineapple, thawed juice concentrate, bananas, and mandarin oranges; mix well.
3. Line muffin tins with paper baking cups. Spoon fruit mixture into paper baking cups (fill each 3/4 full). Cover tightly with plastic wrap, and freeze 2 hours or until firm.
4. Before serving, remove desired number of cups from freezer and let stand 20 minutes to soften slightly. Remove salad from cups and serve on a lettuce leaf if desired.

Cost per Serving

Exchanges

1 Fruit

Calories 85

Calories from Fat 5

Total Fat <1 g

Saturated Fat <1 g

Cholesterol 0 mg

Sodium 11 mg

Carbohydrate 19 g

Dietary Fiber 1 g

Sugars 15 g

Protein 1 g

Apple-Prune Spread

This spread is delicious slathered on toast, waffles, or pancakes. Packaged in a pleasing container, this makes a nice gift.

4 large Granny Smith apples, peeled, cored, and
  sliced

1 12-oz package pitted prunes

1 cup unsweetened apple juice

1 1/2 tsp cinnamon

1/2 tsp allspice

1/2 tsp lemon juice

1. Combine apples, prunes, apple juice, cinnamon, and allspice in a 2-quart saucepan. Bring to a boil over high heat. Reduce heat until fruit is at a simmer and cook for 10 minutes.

2. Uncover and continue cooking, stirring periodically, until fruits are cooked down and most of liquid is absorbed, about 15 minutes. Remove from heat and add lemon juice.

3. Beat with an electric mixer on high speed until smooth. May serve while warm or transfer to storage container, cover tightly, and store in refrigerator—will keep about 3 weeks.

Exchanges

1/2 Fruit

Calories 22

Calories from Fat 0

Total Fat 0 g

Saturated Fat 0 g

Cholesterol 0 mg

Sodium 2 mg

Carbohydrate 5 g

Dietary Fiber <1 g

Sugars 2 g

Protein <1 g

Tropical Slushy

Preparation Time:
  5 minutes

Servings: 4

Serving Size:
  1 cup

Cost per Serving

Banana, pineapple juice, and orange juice contribute a tropical flavor to this icy drink.

1 ripe banana, peeled

1/2 cup unsweetened pineapple juice

1 cup unsweetened orange juice

1 tsp fresh-squeezed lemon juice

1/2 tsp vanilla extract

2 packets NutraSweet artificial sweetener

4 cups ice cubes

1. Combine all ingredients in a blender and blend on high until smooth and slushy. Serve immediately.

Exchanges

1 Fruit

Calories 76

Calories from Fat 0

Total Fat 0 g

Saturated Fat 0 g

Cholesterol 0 mg

Sodium 1 mg

Carbohydrate 18 g

Dietary Fiber 1 g

Sugars 14 g

Protein 1 g

Preparation Time:
5 minutes

Servings: 5

Serving Size:
1 cup

$0.35

Cost per Serving

If you have an herb garden, this beverage can be nicely garnished with fresh mint leaves.

4 chilled fresh peaches, peeled and pitted, OR
    1 chilled 29-oz can peaches in juice, drained
2 cups chilled club soda

1. Place peaches in blender and process until smooth.
2. Pour peach mixture into tall pitcher and add club soda slowly. Stir and serve immediately.

Exchanges

1 Fruit

Calories 48

Calories from Fat 5

Total Fat <1 g

Saturated Fat 0 g

Cholesterol 0 mg

Sodium 28 mg

Carbohydrate 10 g

Dietary Fiber 2 g

Sugars 6 g

Protein 1 g

Berry and Banana Blend

Preparation Time:
10 minutes

Servings: 2

Serving Size:
1 cup

Use leftover blueberries from the Fresh Pears with Berries and "Cream," p. 116.

1/2 cup fat-free (skim) milk

4 ice cubes

1/2 cup fresh or unsweetened frozen blueberries, thawed

1 medium-sized ripe banana, peeled

4 oz sugar-free, fat-free vanilla yogurt

1 tsp vanilla extract

1/8 tsp cinnamon

Cost per Serving

1. Combine milk and ice cubes in a blender, cover, and whip until icy smooth.
2. Add fruit and whip again.
3. Add yogurt, vanilla extract, and cinnamon, then blend until combined. Serve immediately.

Exchanges

1 1/2 Fruit

1/2 Fat-Free Milk

Calories 133

Calories from Fat 9

Total Fat 1 g

Saturated Fat <1 g

Cholesterol 2 mg

Sodium 82 mg

Carbohydrate 26 g

Dietary Fiber 3 g

Sugars 14 g

Protein 5 g

Milk

Servings: 7

Serving Size:
1 cup

$0.21

Cost per Serving

Exchanges

1 1/2 Starch

1/2 Fat-Free Milk

Calories 174

Calories from Fat
18

Total Fat 2 g

Saturated Fat <1 g

Cholesterol 2 mg

Sodium 342 mg

Carbohydrate 33 g

Dietary Fiber <1 g

Sugars 5 g

Protein 6 g

Savory Potato Soup

It's the perfect warm-up on a chilly winter's evening—and it's great reheated for lunch too!

5 cups peeled and cubed potatoes

3 cups fat-free (skim) milk

1 cup water

3 cubes reduced-sodium chicken bouillon

1 cup finely chopped onion

1/2 cup finely chopped celery

1 Tbsp reduced-calorie margarine

3/4 tsp salt

1/4 tsp ground black pepper

1/8 tsp garlic powder

1. Place potatoes in a large Dutch oven, cover with water, and cook over medium-high heat until potatoes are tender when pierced with a fork (about 15 minutes). Drain off water.

2. Remove approximately half of potatoes, mash with a potato masher, then return to pan.

3. Add milk, 1 cup water, bouillon, onion, celery, margarine, salt, pepper, and garlic powder to potatoes. Simmer uncovered for 30 minutes or until thickened and heated through. Stir periodically to prevent sticking.

Purple Cow Pops

Preparation Time:
10 minutes

Servings: 5

Serving Size:
1 pop

Creamy grape pops—it can't get any easier than two ingredients!

2 8-oz containers sugar-free, fat-free vanilla yogurt

1/4 cup + 2 Tbsp unsweetened frozen grape juice concentrate, thawed

1. In a mixing bowl, combine yogurt and grape juice concentrate; stir well.
2. Pour into small frozen-pop molds or 5-oz wax-coated paper cups, filling 3/4 full, and freeze solid (about 2 hours). If using paper cups, partially freeze (about 1 hour) then insert Popsicle sticks. Tear off cups when frozen solid.

$0.26

Cost per Serving

Exchanges

1/2 Fruit

1/2 Fat-Free Milk

Calories 81

Calories from Fat 5

Total Fat <1 g

Saturated Fat <1 g

Cholesterol 2 mg

Sodium 78 mg

Carbohydrate 15 g

Dietary Fiber <1 g

Sugars 14 g

Protein 4 g

Strawberry Whip

$0.43

Cost per Serving

Use as a creamy, light dessert or as a dip for fresh fruit.

2 8-oz containers sugar-free, fat-free strawberry yogurt

1 8-oz container frozen fat-free whipped topping, thawed

1/2 cup crushed fresh or unsweetened thawed frozen strawberries

1. Place all ingredients in a large mixing bowl and stir together. Cover and chill if not serving immediately.

2. Serve in individual glass dishes garnished with a fresh strawberry.

3. For a frosty dessert, pour into an 8 × 8-inch pan, freeze for 2 1/2 hours, thaw slightly, cut into 6 squares, and garnish each square with a fresh strawberry.

Exchanges

1 Fat-Free Milk

Calories 93

Calories from Fat 5

Total Fat <1 g

Saturated Fat <1 g

Cholesterol 2 mg

Sodium 84 mg

Carbohydrate 19 g

Dietary Fiber 1 g

Sugars 7 g

Protein 3 g

Caribbean Sunrise Smoothie

Preparation Time:
  5 minutes

Servings: 4

Serving Size:
  1 cup

Put fruit in the freezer the night before so that you can whip this breakfast drink together quickly. Transfer pineapple to a covered plastic container before freezing. If the pineapple is frozen solid by morning, thaw slightly for a few seconds in the microwave.

Cost per Serving

1 small peeled ripe banana, frozen

1 8-oz can crushed pineapple in juice, frozen until slushy

2 8-oz containers sugar-free, fat-free coconut cream pie yogurt

1/2 cup unsweetened orange juice

1. Place all ingredients in blender and whip until smooth.

Exchanges

1 Fruit

1/2 Fat-Free Milk

Calories 117

Calories from Fat 5

Total Fat <1 g

Saturated Fat <1 g

Cholesterol 3 mg

Sodium 96 mg

Carbohydrate 22 g

Dietary Fiber 2 g

Sugars 17 g

Protein 6 g

Preparation Time:
5 minutes

Servings: 4

Serving Size:
1 cup

$0.26

Cost per Serving

Exchanges

1 1/2 Fat-Free Milk

Calories 126

Calories from Fat
18

Total Fat 2 g

Saturated Fat <1 g

Cholesterol 5 mg

Sodium 155 mg

Carbohydrate 18 g

Dietary Fiber 1 g

Sugars 12 g

Protein 9 g

Hot Chocolate with Peppermint Whipped Topping

The whipped topping's hint of peppermint pleasantly complements this steaming chocolate drink.

1/4 cup instant sugar-free chocolate milk mix

32 oz fat-free (skim) milk

Topping

3 drops (1/16 tsp) peppermint extract

1 drop red food coloring

1/2 cup frozen "lite" whipped topping, thawed

1. Combine chocolate milk mix and milk in a large saucepan; whisk until mix is dissolved. Heat uncovered over medium heat until milk is hot; stir frequently to prevent scorching—do not boil.

2. In a small mixing bowl, whisk together extract, food coloring, and whipped topping.

3. Pour hot chocolate into 4 mugs, and top each with 2 Tbsp peppermint whipped topping.

Cinnamon-Honey Eggnog

Preparation Time:
  5 minutes

Servings: 7

Serving Size:
  1 cup

Cost per Serving

You may garnish each mug with a twist of orange peel and a sprinkle of cinnamon. Before measuring the honey for this recipe, try coating the measuring spoon with cooking spray to prevent the honey from sticking to it.

6 cups fat-free (skim) milk

1 cup liquid egg substitute

5 Tbsp honey

1 1/2 tsp vanilla extract

1/4 tsp ground cinnamon

1. Combine milk, egg substitute, and honey in a large pan, mixing well. Place over medium heat and cook for 15 minutes or until eggnog becomes frothy on top and bubbles gently. When eggnog becomes warm, whisk frequently to prevent scorching. Remove pan from heat.

2. Stir in vanilla extract and cinnamon. Chill eggnog at least 3 hours before serving—will thicken slightly upon chilling.

Exchanges

1 Fruit

1/2 Fat-Free Milk

1 Very Lean Meat

Calories 138

Calories from Fat
  18

Total Fat 2 g

Saturated Fat <1 g

Cholesterol 4 mg

Sodium 172 mg

Carbohydrate 19 g

Dietary Fiber <1 g

Sugars 9 g

Protein 11 g

Meat and Others

Preparation Time:
45 minutes

Servings: 10

Serving Size:
1 piece chicken

Cost per Serving

Exchanges

1/2 Starch

3 Lean Meat

Calories 187

Calories from Fat
63

Total Fat 7 g

Saturated Fat 2 g

Cholesterol 69 mg

Sodium 221 mg

Carbohydrate 7 g

Dietary Fiber <1 g

Sugars <1 g

Protein 24 g

Marilyn's Spicy "Fried" Chicken

This is a great recipe to use for planned-overs. Dice extra chicken and toss with fresh lettuce, tomato, cucumber, mushrooms, onion, and low-fat dressing for a refreshing salad, or stuff it in a pita pocket for a sandwich with a twist.

1 whole fryer chicken (around 4 lb)

3 egg whites

1 0.4-oz packet ranch-style salad dressing mix

1/2 tsp ground black pepper

3/4 cup dry unseasoned bread crumbs

Cooking spray

1 Tbsp corn oil

1. Preheat oven to 375°F. Cut the chicken into 10 pieces, then remove skin and fat. Rinse chicken pieces under warm water and lay on paper towels to drain.

2. Place egg whites in a large bowl and mix well with wire whisk. In a large zip-top plastic bag, combine salad dressing mix, pepper, and bread crumbs. Dip each piece of chicken in egg whites to coat, then place in bag of seasonings and shake until well coated.

3. Lay chicken on baking sheet coated with cooking spray, and sprinkle with remaining seasoned crumbs. Spray chicken with cooking spray, and bake for 40 minutes. Brush with corn oil, and bake 10 minutes longer or until chicken is tender and no longer pink.*

*Before serving, reserve the breast if you want to prepare Southwestern Chicken Wrap-Ups this week.

Southwestern Chicken Wrap-Ups

Preparation Time:
20 minutes

Servings: 5

Serving Size:
2 wrap-ups

Combine small leftover amounts of rice, corn, black beans, and chicken for a delicious meal! Salsa and fat-free sour cream make great toppers for these wrap-ups.

Cost per Serving

Cooking spray

1/4 cup finely diced green pepper

1/4 cup finely diced onion

1 cup cooked white rice

1 cup corn OR 1 8 3/4-oz can corn, drained

1/2 15-oz can black beans, drained and rinsed, OR 1 cup cooked dried black beans

1 Tbsp Red Hot sauce

Breast (bones removed) from Marilyn's Spicy "Fried" Chicken OR substitute 1 8-oz boneless, skinless grilled chicken breast, thinly sliced and warmed

10 flour tortillas, warmed

1/2 cup + 2 Tbsp salsa

Fat-free sour cream, optional

Exchanges

4 Starch

1 Vegetable

2 Very Lean Meat

1/2 Fat

Calories 432

Calories from Fat 72

Total Fat 8 g

Saturated Fat 1 g

Cholesterol 39 mg

Sodium 730 mg

Carbohydrate 65 g

Dietary Fiber 6 g

Sugars 2 g

Protein 25 g

1. In a small nonstick skillet coated with cooking spray, sauté green pepper and onion over medium heat until onion turns clear (about 3 minutes).

2. Add rice, corn, beans, and Red Hot sauce to pepper and onion—toss to combine. Warm over low-medium heat for 5 minutes.

3. Divide rice mixture and chicken evenly among the 10 tortillas (approximately 1/3 cup filling per tortilla), spreading down the center. Roll up each tortilla, placing seam-side down on plate, and drizzle with 1 Tbsp salsa.

Cost per Serving

Italian Chicken Skillet

Cut up one whole chicken (about 4 lb)—you can use the breast in this recipe and the remaining pieces to make Oven-Barbecued Chicken.

Cooking spray

1 tsp corn oil

1 tsp (or 1 clove) minced garlic

1/4 cup diced onion

1 whole chicken breast (approximately 8 oz), skin and bones removed, diced into bite-sized pieces

1 7-oz can mushroom stems and pieces, drained and rinsed

1 small zucchini squash, quartered lengthwise and diced into bite-sized pieces

1 14-oz jar spaghetti sauce

1/2 cup water

1/8 tsp red pepper flakes

4 cups cooked pasta

Exchanges

3 Starch

3 Vegetable (or
1 Carbohydrate)

2 Lean Meat

1/2 Fat

Calories 441

Calories from Fat
81

Total Fat 9 g

Saturated Fat 1 g

Cholesterol 67 mg

Sodium 808 mg

Carbohydrate 62 g

Dietary Fiber 6 g

Sugars 4 g

Protein 28 g

1. Coat a large nonstick skillet with cooking spray. Add oil and warm over medium heat. Add garlic and onion. Cook until onion turns clear (about 3 minutes), stirring frequently.

2. Add chicken and cook until no longer pink (about 7 minutes). Stir in mushrooms, zucchini, spaghetti sauce, water, and red pepper flakes.

3. Reduce heat to low, cover, and cook for 10 minutes, stirring periodically. Serve over hot pasta.

Oven-Barbecued Chicken

Preparation Time:
30 minutes

Servings: 8

Serving Size:
1 piece

Cut up one whole chicken (about 4 lb)—you can use the breasts to make Italian Chicken Skillet and the remaining pieces to make this recipe.

Cost per Serving

Barbecue Sauce (makes 1 1/2 cups)

1/4 cup white vinegar

1/4 cup water

1 Tbsp corn oil

1/2 cup ketchup

3 Tbsp Worcestershire sauce

2 Tbsp finely diced onion

2 Tbsp brown sugar (light or dark)

1/8 tsp garlic powder

2 tsp dry mustard

1/4 tsp salt

1/8 tsp coarse ground black pepper

1 chicken (approximately 4 lb) cut up into
    10 pieces with skin removed—reserve split
    breast for another use

Cooking spray

Exchanges

1/2 Carbohydrate

2 Lean Meat

1. Preheat oven to 350°F. Combine all sauce ingredients in a small saucepan and simmer for 15 minutes over low-medium heat, stirring occasionally.
2. Place chicken in a 13 × 9 × 2-inch baking dish coated with cooking spray. Cover chicken evenly with 1 cup barbecue sauce.
3. Bake for 1 to 1 1/2 hours (or until chicken is tender and no longer pink), basting periodically with remaining sauce.

Calories 159

Calories from Fat
    63

Total Fat 7 g

Saturated Fat 2 g

Cholesterol 50 mg

Sodium 313 mg

Carbohydrate 9 g

Dietary Fiber <1 g

Sugars 1 g

Protein 15 g

Preparation Time:
40 minutes

Servings: 12

Serving Size:
1 cup

Cost per Serving

Exchanges

1 1/2 Starch

1 Very Lean Meat

Calories 157

Calories from Fat 9

Total Fat 1 g

Saturated Fat <1 g

Cholesterol 19 mg

Sodium 472 mg

Carbohydrate 27 g

Dietary Fiber 1 g

Sugars 5 g

Protein 10 g

Classic Chicken and Dumplings

Cut up one whole chicken (about 4 lb)—you can use the breast to make Chinese Chicken Soup, p. 138, and the remaining pieces in this recipe.

1 cut-up chicken (about 4 lb)—reserve the breast for another use

3 quarts water

2 cubes reduced-sodium chicken bouillon

1 medium onion, finely chopped

2 ribs celery, finely diced

1 carrot, peeled and finely diced

1/4 tsp garlic powder

3/4 tsp salt

1/4 tsp ground black pepper

1 tsp dried parsley flakes

1/4 cup all-purpose flour

1 cup cold water

Dumplings

3 cups biscuit mix

1 cup fat-free (skim) milk

1. Place chicken, 3 quarts water, bouillon, onion, celery, and carrot in a 2-gallon stockpot. Cover and bring to boil over high heat. Reduce heat to medium and cook for 30 minutes or until meat is tender and pulls away from the bone.

2. Remove chicken from broth. Skim fat from top of broth. Discard fat. Debone chicken. Discard skin and bones, shred meat, and return shredded meat to defatted broth.

DIABETES MEALS ON $7 A DAY—OR LESS!

3. Add garlic powder, salt, pepper, and parsley and return to boil over high heat.

4. In a liquid measuring cup, dissolve flour in 1 cup cold water, whisking well. Add to boiling liquid and stir until slightly thickened.

5. Place biscuit mix and milk in a medium mixing bowl and stir to combine. Drop by tablespoons into boiling liquid. Reduce heat to medium, cover pot, and simmer for 20 minutes or until dumplings are fluffy; gently stir periodically.

$0.33

Cost per Serving

Exchanges

1 Starch

1 Very Lean Meat

Calories 101

Calories from Fat 9

Total Fat 1 g

Saturated Fat <1 g

Cholesterol 21 mg

Sodium 294 mg

Carbohydrate 13 g

Dietary Fiber 1 g

Sugars 1 g

Protein 10 g

Chinese Chicken Soup

Cut up one whole chicken (about 4 lb)—use the breast in this soup and the remaining pieces to make Classic Chicken and Dumplings, p. 136.

1 whole chicken breast (approximately 8 oz total), skin removed

8 cups water

2 cubes reduced-sodium chicken bouillon

1/2 cup uncooked medium-grain rice

1 cup finely diced celery (3 ribs)

1 cup finely diced onion (1 large onion)

1 7-oz can mushroom stems and pieces, drained

2 Tbsp reduced-sodium soy sauce

1/4 tsp garlic powder

1/8 tsp salt

1/8 tsp ground black pepper

1. In a 1-gallon stockpot, place chicken, water, and bouillon. Cover and bring to a boil over high heat. Simmer chicken about 20 minutes or until it is no longer pink.

2. Remove chicken from liquid; remove the meat from the bone and shred it. Return shredded meat to liquid.

3. Add remaining ingredients and simmer uncovered over medium heat for 20 minutes or until rice is tender.

Sesame Chicken and Vegetables

This recipe incorporates canned chicken to simplify preparation and shorten cooking time.

1 cup uncooked medium-grain rice
1 head broccoli (8 oz)
1 Tbsp corn oil
2 carrots, peeled and cut into matchsticks
1 large onion, coarsely chopped
1 7-oz can mushroom stems and pieces, drained
1 tsp (or 1 clove) minced garlic
1 10-oz can 96% fat-free chunk chicken in water, drained
1 cup fat-free reduced-sodium chicken broth
2 Tbsp reduced-sodium soy sauce
1 tsp cornstarch
1/4 tsp ground ginger
1 tsp sesame seeds, lightly toasted

1. Cook rice according to package directions, omitting fat and salt.

2. Portion broccoli head into bite-sized florets. Peel broccoli stem and slice into bite-sized pieces.

3. In a large nonstick skillet, warm oil over high heat. Add broccoli, carrots, onion, mushrooms, and garlic. Cook, stirring frequently, for 3 minutes. Reduce heat to medium, add chicken, cover skillet, and cook until vegetables are crisp-tender, about 4 minutes.

4. In a small bowl, combine broth, soy sauce, cornstarch, and ginger. Whisk until mixed. Pour into vegetable/chicken mixture and cook, stirring frequently, until sauce thickens slightly, about 1 minute. Cook an additional 2 minutes.

5. Spoon over cooked rice, sprinkle with toasted sesame seeds, and serve immediately.

Preparation Time: 15 minutes

Servings: 6

Serving Size: 1 cup meat mixture, 1/2 cup rice

$0.97

Cost per Serving

Exchanges

2 Starch

1 Vegetable

1 Lean Meat

Calories 241

Calories from Fat 45

Total Fat 5 g

Saturated Fat 1 g

Cholesterol 23 mg

Sodium 481 mg

Carbohydrate 35 g

Dietary Fiber 3 g

Sugars 3 g

Protein 14 g

Tempting Turkey Pot Pie

Preparation Time:
25 minutes

Servings: 7

Serving Size:
1 cup

$0.36

Cost per Serving

Exchanges

3 Starch

1 Very Lean Meat

Calories 280

Calories from Fat
36

Total Fat 4 g

Saturated Fat 1 g

Cholesterol 35 mg

Sodium 692 mg

Carbohydrate 42 g

Dietary Fiber 2 g

Sugars 8 g

Protein 19 g

Plan to cook Golden Roasted Turkey Breast, p. 142, earlier in the week and use leftovers for this pot pie!

3 Tbsp reduced-calorie stick margarine

1/3 cup all-purpose flour

1/2 tsp salt

1/8 tsp garlic powder

1/8 tsp ground black pepper

2 cups water

3/4 cup fat-free (skim) milk

2 cubes reduced-sodium chicken bouillon

1 8 1/2-oz can peas and carrots, drained and rinsed

1 8 3/4-oz can corn, drained and rinsed

1 small onion, finely diced

2 cups (about 10 oz) shredded turkey breast

Cooking spray

Topping

2 cups biscuit mix

2/3 cup fat-free (skim) milk

1. Preheat oven to 400°F. Melt margarine in a large saucepan over medium heat. Stir in flour, salt, garlic powder, and pepper—a thick paste will form. Add water, milk, and bouillon cubes—stir with a wire whisk until mixture thickens slightly.

140   DIABETES MEALS ON $7 A DAY—OR LESS!

2. Add peas and carrots, corn, onion, and turkey. Stir to combine. Spoon into a 2-quart casserole coated with cooking spray and set aside.

3. Place biscuit mix and milk in a mixing bowl, then stir to combine. Drop dough by rounded tablespoons onto top of turkey mixture. Bake uncovered for 30 minutes or until biscuit topping is golden and filling is bubbly.

$0.22

Cost per Serving

Golden Roasted Turkey Breast

Turkey breast is excellent for a dinner party or a holiday meal. Leftovers make yummy sandwiches or can be incorporated into Tempting Turkey Pot Pie, p. 140!

1/4 tsp onion powder

1/4 tsp garlic powder

1/4 tsp coarse ground black pepper

1/4 tsp salt

1 uncooked turkey breast (about 5 lb), thaw if frozen

1 Tbsp all-purpose flour

1 roasting bag

1. Preheat oven to 350°F. In a small bowl, combine onion powder, garlic powder, pepper, and salt—set aside.

2. Rinse turkey and pat dry. Loosen skin with knife, then cut skin down one side of turkey breast. Pull skin aside, sprinkle turkey with seasonings, and replace skin.

3. Place flour in roasting bag and shake to coat. Add turkey to roasting bag and close bag using nylon tie that accompanies it. Cut six 1/2-inch slits in top of bag to allow steam to escape. Insert meat thermometer into breast through one of the slits in the bag.

4. Bake approximately 2 hours or until the meat thermometer registers at least 170°F—the meat should be tender and no longer pink. Remove from oven and allow meat to stand 20 minutes before slicing—discard skin.

Exchanges

4 Very Lean Meat

Calories 134

Calories from Fat 9

Total Fat 1 g

Saturated Fat <1 g

Cholesterol 94 mg

Sodium 88 mg

Carbohydrate <1 g

Dietary Fiber <1 g

Sugars <1 g

Protein 30 g

Spunky Spaghetti Sauce

Here's a versatile meat sauce that can be served over steaming spaghetti or any hot pasta. It even works in lasagna!

1 lb ground chuck

1 tsp (or 1 clove) minced garlic

2 Tbsp dried parsley

1 tsp dried basil

1 tsp dried crushed oregano

1 tsp salt

4 dashes Red Hot sauce

4 Tbsp Worcestershire sauce

2 15-oz cans tomato sauce

1 6-oz can tomato paste

1 14.5-oz can diced tomatoes

1. In a large skillet, brown ground chuck over medium-high heat, then drain well.
2. Add remaining ingredients and simmer, covered, for 30 minutes. Stir often.

$0.58

Cost per Serving

Exchanges

3 Vegetable (or 1 Carbohydrate)

3 Lean Meat

Calories 229

Calories from Fat 81

Total Fat 9 g

Saturated Fat 4 g

Cholesterol 56 mg

Sodium 461 mg

Carbohydrate 17 g

Dietary Fiber 3 g

Sugars 3 g

Protein 20 g

Servings: 6

**Serving Size:
3 slices**

Cost per Serving

Exchanges

1/2 Starch

3 Vegetable (or 1
Carbohydrate)

3 Lean Meat

1/2 Fat

Calories 309

Calories from Fat
117

Total Fat 13 g

Saturated Fat 5 g

Cholesterol 75 mg

Sodium 356 mg

Carbohydrate 22 g

Dietary Fiber 4 g

Sugars 6 g

Protein 26 g

Stuffed Pepper Slices

*This unique version of stuffed peppers is a great
way to use leftover rice or corn.*

6 medium-sized green peppers

1 lb ground chuck

1 cup cooked rice or corn

1 small onion, finely diced

1/4 cup fat-free (skim) milk

1/8 tsp ground black pepper

1/4 tsp salt

Cooking spray

1 15-oz can tomato sauce

1. Cut tops from peppers and discard. Remove
   seeds, then set peppers aside.

2. In a large bowl, combine ground chuck, rice or
   corn, onion, milk, pepper, and salt; mixing well.
   Stuff peppers with meat mixture, cover, and
   refrigerate for at least 2 hours.

3. Preheat oven to 350°F. Remove peppers from
   refrigerator and cut each into 3 slices. Arrange
   overlapping slices in 9 × 13-inch baking dish
   coated with cooking spray, and top with tomato
   sauce.

4. Cover with foil and bake for 45 minutes.
   Remove foil and continue baking an additional
   15 minutes.

Mexican Scramble

Preparation Time:
15 minutes

Servings: 6

Serving Size:
1 cup

This simple and spicy stovetop meal is a great way to use a remaining small serving of macaroni or other pasta.

Cost per Serving

1 lb ground chuck

1 large onion, chopped

1/2 green pepper, diced

1 15.25-oz can corn, drained and rinsed

1 10-oz can tomatoes and green chilies

1 8-oz can tomato sauce

1/4 tsp salt

1/8 tsp ground black pepper

1 tsp to 1 Tbsp chili powder, according to taste

1 cup cooked macaroni (or any small pasta)

1 Tbsp cornstarch dissolved in

1/4 cup cold water

1. In a large skillet over medium heat, brown and drain ground chuck.
2. Add onion, green pepper, corn, tomatoes and green chilies, tomato sauce, salt, pepper, and chili powder; mix well. Cook uncovered over medium heat for 15 minutes; stir periodically.
3. Add macaroni and cornstarch dissolved in water; stir well. Continue cooking and stirring over medium heat until mixture thickens, about 2 to 3 minutes.

Exchanges

1 1/2 Starch

1 Vegetable

3 Lean Meat

1/2 Fat

Calories 329

Calories from Fat 117

Total Fat 13 g

Saturated Fat 5 g

Cholesterol 75 mg

Sodium 548 mg

Carbohydrate 27 g

Dietary Fiber 3 g

Sugars 5 g

Protein 26 g

Beef and Broccoli Stroganoff

Preparation Time:
20 minutes

Servings: 5

Serving Size:
1 cup meat,
1 cup noodles

$1.24

Cost per Serving

Exchanges

3 1/2 Starch

1 Vegetable

3 Lean Meat

Calories 463

Calories from Fat
99

Total Fat 11 g

Saturated Fat 2 g

Cholesterol 57 mg

Sodium 538 mg

Carbohydrate 52 g

Dietary Fiber 7 g

Sugars 5 g

Protein 39 g

Crisp-tender broccoli adds color and enhances the flavor of traditional beef stroganoff.

1 lb round steak, partially frozen

6 Tbsp all-purpose flour, divided

Cooking spray

1 Tbsp corn oil

1 clove (or 1 tsp) garlic, minced

1 cup fresh sliced mushrooms

1 small onion, finely diced

2 Tbsp reduced-calorie margarine

3/4 tsp salt

1/4 tsp ground black pepper

1 cube reduced-sodium beef bouillon dissolved in

1 1/2 cups warm water

1 cup fat-free sour cream

2 cups lightly steamed small broccoli florets

5 cups cooked cholesterol-free egg noodles

1. Remove fat from meat, and slice meat across the grain into bite-sized pieces. Place 3 Tbsp flour in a large zip-top plastic bag. Add meat in two batches and shake to coat.

2. In a large nonstick skillet coated with cooking spray, heat corn oil over medium heat. Add meat and brown on both sides. Add garlic, mushrooms, and onion, then cook for 5 minutes. Add margarine and cook until melted.

3. Stir in 2 Tbsp flour until liquid forms a paste. Stir in salt, pepper, and bouillon dissolved in water. Continue cooking 10 minutes; stirring frequently.

4. Stir remaining 1 Tbsp flour into sour cream, then add to meat mixture. Cook for 5 minutes, stirring frequently, but do not boil.

5. Toss in steamed broccoli, spoon over noodles, and serve immediately.

Cost per Serving

Exchanges

1 Starch

3 Very Lean Meat

Calories 188

Calories from Fat
36

Total Fat 4 g

Saturated Fat 1 g

Cholesterol 55 mg

Sodium 655 mg

Carbohydrate 13 g

Dietary Fiber 1 g

Sugars 2 g

Protein 25 g

Stovetop Swiss Steak

Try mashed potatoes as a tasty accompaniment!

Cooking spray

1 lb round steak, cut into 4 equal portions with fat removed

1 8-oz can tomato sauce

1/3 cup water

1 Tbsp Worcestershire sauce

1/4 cup diced onion

1/2 tsp salt

1/8 tsp ground black pepper

1/2 tsp crushed oregano

1 Tbsp dried parsley flakes

1 8.5-oz can peas, drained and rinsed

1. Warm a large nonstick skillet coated with cooking spray over medium-high heat. Add steak and brown on both sides. Drain off any fat.

2. In a small bowl, combine tomato sauce, water, Worcestershire sauce, onion, salt, pepper, oregano, and parsley; mix well. Pour over meat in skillet, cover, and simmer for 30 minutes or until meat is tender.

3. Gently stir in peas and cook an additional 2 to 3 minutes until peas are thoroughly heated.

Bountiful Beef Stew

Preparation Time:
30 minutes

Servings: 10

Serving Size:
1 cup

Cost per Serving

This hearty, filling stew uses one of the least expensive cuts of meat.

1 46-oz can tomato juice

3 cups water

2 cubes reduced-sodium beef bouillon

1 lb stew beef, cut into 1-inch cubes, fat trimmed (may substitute leftover round steak or beef roast)

1 large onion, coarsely chopped

2 large carrots, peeled and diced

3 medium potatoes, peeled and cubed

1/8 tsp ground black pepper

1 Tbsp flour dissolved in

1/4 cup cold water

1. In a 1-gallon pot, combine tomato juice, 3 cups water, bouillon cubes, stew beef, onion, carrots, and potatoes. Cover and bring to a boil over medium-high heat.
2. Decrease heat until stew is at a simmer, and cook for 45 minutes, stirring periodically.
3. Add pepper and flour dissolved in water, stir to combine, then simmer uncovered 15 minutes more.

Exchanges

1/2 Starch

2 Vegetable

1 Very Lean Meat

Calories 138

Calories from Fat 18

Total Fat 2 g

Saturated Fat 1 g

Cholesterol 22 mg

Sodium 440 mg

Carbohydrate 20 g

Dietary Fiber 2 g

Sugars 5 g

Protein 10 g

Western Frittata

Cost per Serving

*A frittata is an Italian omelet in which the "fillings" are combined with the eggs **before** the eggs are cooked. Any leftover meats or vegetables can be substituted for the ground chuck and vegetables in this recipe.*

1/2 lb ground chuck

1/2 medium onion, finely chopped

1/2 green pepper, finely diced

1/4 tsp seasoned salt

1/4 tsp ground black pepper

2 Tbsp reduced-calorie margarine

1 2-lb bag frozen shredded hash brown potatoes, thawed

1/4 tsp salt

1 egg + 4 egg whites

1/3 cup fat-free (skim) milk

1 cup (4 oz) finely shredded reduced-fat cheddar cheese

Exchanges

2 Starch

1 Vegetable

2 Medium-Fat Meat

Calories 344

Calories from Fat
108

Total Fat 12 g

Saturated Fat 5 g

Cholesterol 87 mg

Sodium 419 mg

Carbohydrate 36 g

Dietary Fiber 4 g

Sugars 4 g

Protein 23 g

1. In a 12-inch nonstick skillet, brown ground chuck along with onion and green pepper. Drain well. Stir in seasoned salt and pepper. Remove meat mixture from skillet and set aside. Wipe drippings from skillet.

2. Add margarine to skillet and melt over low heat. Add hash brown potatoes. Sprinkle evenly with salt and toss to coat. Spread potatoes evenly over bottom of skillet. Spread meat mixture evenly over potatoes.

3. In a small bowl, combine egg, egg whites, and milk; whisk well. Pour evenly over ingredients in skillet. Cover and cook over low heat about 20 minutes or until potatoes are tender.

4. Sprinkle evenly with cheese, cover, and cook an additional 5 minutes or until cheese is melted. Cut into 6 equal wedges and serve immediately.

Dijon-Crusted Beef Roast

Dijon mustard and seasoned bread crumbs create a unique crust for this succulent roast.

1 2.5-lb boneless chuck roast, fat trimmed
Butter-flavored cooking spray
1/2 cup dry unseasoned bread crumbs
2 Tbsp dried parsley flakes
1/2 tsp ground black pepper
1/2 tsp salt
2 tsp (or 2 cloves) minced garlic
1/4 cup Dijon mustard

1. Preheat oven to 325°F. Place roast in a roasting pan coated with cooking spray.
2. In a small bowl, combine bread crumbs, parsley, pepper, and salt.
3. In another small bowl, mix together garlic and mustard. Spread mustard mixture on top and sides of roast.
4. Firmly pat bread crumb mixture onto mustard. Spray top and sides of roast with cooking spray. Insert meat thermometer into center of roast. Cover with foil and bake for 2 hours.
5. Remove foil and continue baking an additional 30 minutes or until crust is lightly browned, meat thermometer registers 170°F, and meat is no longer pink.
6. Remove from oven and let stand 20 minutes before slicing.

Egg in a Basket

Preparation Time:
  5 minutes

Servings: 4

**Serving Size: 1 egg
  in a basket**

Cost per Serving

Lightly toast the leftover bread circles, then sprinkle them with cinnamon or top them with 100% fruit spread.

Butter-flavored cooking spray

4 slices whole-wheat bread

4 medium eggs

4 dashes salt

4 dashes ground black pepper

1. Coat a large nonstick skillet and both sides of the bread slices with cooking spray. Place bread in skillet, invert a 2-inch glass over the center of each slice, and cut out a circle. Set circles aside. Heat bread slices over low-medium heat.
2. Break 1 egg into center of each bread slice, and sprinkle with a dash of salt and a dash of pepper. Cook until egg white begins to turn white (about 3 minutes). Turn bread/egg with spatula and continue cooking until egg yolk is firm (about 3 more minutes).

Exchanges

1 Starch

1 Medium-Fat Meat

Calories 151

Calories from Fat
  63

Total Fat 7 g

Saturated Fat 2 g

Cholesterol 212
  mg

Sodium 316 mg

Carbohydrate 13 g

Dietary Fiber 3 g

Sugars 1 g

Protein 9 g

Pineapple-Glazed Ham Steaks

Cost per Serving

Purchase a fully cooked boneless ham, slice off 4 steaks for this recipe, then dice the remaining ham into bite-sized pieces and freeze them in 1-cup amounts in zip-top plastic bags for use in soups.

1/3 cup barbecue sauce

1 8-oz can crushed pineapple in juice, undrained

4 4-oz fully cooked ham steaks or cutlets

1. Combine barbecue sauce and pineapple in a shallow dish; stir well. Add ham steaks and spoon sauce over to coat. Cover and refrigerate at least 1 hour to allow flavors to blend. Remove ham and reserve marinade.

2. Grill ham over hot coals 3 minutes. Turn steaks over and grill an additional 3 minutes or until heated through. Baste with reserved marinade during cooking. (Ham may also be cooked under broiler, 3 inches from heat source, 3 minutes per side.)

Exchanges

1 Carbohydrate

4 Very Lean Meat

1/2 Fat

Calories 239

Calories from Fat 63

Total Fat 7 g

Saturated Fat 2 g

Cholesterol 62 mg

Sodium 1,809 mg

Carbohydrate 15 g

Dietary Fiber <1 g

Sugars 8 g

Protein 29 g

Asian Pork Stir-Fry

Preparation Time:
20 minutes

Servings: 4

Serving Size:
1 cup

Cost per Serving

To stretch this stir-fry to feed more people, cut the serving size in half and serve over hot rice.

Cooking spray

8 oz raw pork, cubed (can use meat from any cut with fat trimmed off)

1 carrot, peeled and thinly sliced

2 potatoes, diced (skin on)

1 small onion, diced

1 cup diced celery

2 cups shredded green cabbage

Sauce

1 Tbsp cornstarch

1/3 cup cold water

1/4 cup reduced-sodium soy sauce

1/4 cup ketchup

2 Tbsp brown sugar

1. Coat a large nonstick skillet with cooking spray. Add pork and cook over medium-high heat, stirring frequently, until meat is browned.

2. Add carrot and potatoes and cook 5 minutes, stirring often. Add onion, celery, and cabbage and cook 5 more minutes or until potato is tender; toss frequently.

3. In a small bowl, combine cornstarch and water, whisking until cornstarch is dissolved. Add soy sauce, ketchup, and brown sugar, mixing well.

4. Pour sauce over stir-fry and toss to coat. Reduce heat to low and simmer for 10 minutes.

Exchanges

2 Starch

1 Vegetable

2 Lean Meat

Calories 304

Calories from Fat 72

Total Fat 8 g

Saturated Fat 3 g

Cholesterol 52 mg

Sodium 779 mg

Carbohydrate 37 g

Dietary Fiber 3 g

Sugars 4 g

Protein 21 g

Preparation Time:
10 minutes

Servings: 4

Serving Size:
4 oz

Cost per Serving

Exchanges

1/2 Starch

4 Very Lean Meat

Calories 165

Calories from Fat
45

Total Fat 5 g

Saturated Fat 1 g

Cholesterol 158
mg

Sodium 233 mg

Carbohydrate 7 g

Dietary Fiber <1 g

Sugars 0 g

Protein 23 g

Seasoned Pan-Fried Catfish

Instant potato flakes lend a crunchy coating to the tender catfish fillets.

1/2 cup instant potato flakes

1/2 tsp seasoned salt

1/8 tsp ground black pepper

1 lb catfish fillets

1 egg, beaten

Butter-flavored cooking spray

1. In a shallow dish, combine potato flakes, seasoned salt, and pepper. Dip catfish fillets in beaten egg, then coat well with seasoned potato mixture.

2. Place in a large nonstick skillet coated generously with cooking spray, and cook over medium heat until fillets are golden, about 10 minutes.

3. Spray remaining uncooked side of fillets with cooking spray, turn over, and continue cooking until golden and fish flakes easily with a fork (about 10 more minutes). Turn only once during cooking.

Mediterranean Tuna Toss

Preparation Time:
  10 minutes

Servings: 8

Serving Size:
  1 cup

Serve leftovers as a tasty, cool pasta salad.

8 oz uncooked medium pasta shells

1 tsp corn oil

1 tsp (or 1 clove) minced garlic

1 28-oz can diced tomatoes

1/4 tsp dried thyme

1/4 tsp dried oregano

1/4 tsp ground black pepper

1 12-oz can tuna in water, drained and flaked

1/2 cup diced green onion

1/2 cup (about 2 oz) crumbled feta cheese

$0.49

Cost per Serving

1. Cook pasta shells according to package directions, but omit salt. Drain, cover, and set aside.

2. Meanwhile, in a large nonstick skillet, warm oil over medium heat. Add garlic and cook for 2 minutes, stirring to prevent browning. Add tomatoes, thyme, oregano, and pepper. Simmer uncovered over medium heat for 5 minutes.

3. Stir in tuna and green onion, then cook an additional 5 minutes or until heated through.

4. Place pasta in a serving dish. Add tuna mixture and toss to coat. Sprinkle with cheese and serve immediately.

Exchanges

1 1/2 Starch

1 Vegetable

2 Very Lean Meat

Calories 229

Calories from Fat
  45

Total Fat 5 g

Saturated Fat 3 g

Cholesterol 14 mg

Sodium 660 mg

Carbohydrate 27 g

Dietary Fiber 1 g

Sugars 4 g

Protein 19 g

Gourmet Grilled Cheese

$0.63

Cost per Serving

Here's a calcium boost for those who aren't "milk-drinkers"!

4 slices whole-wheat bread

8 tsp reduced-calorie stick margarine, room temperature

Cooking spray

4 large tomato slices

2 slices fat-free processed American cheese

12 thin, large zucchini slices

1/8 tsp seasoned salt

Ground black pepper

Exchanges

2 Starch

1 Lean Meat

1 Vegetable

1 Fat

Calories 279

Calories from Fat 99

Total Fat 11 g

Saturated Fat 1 g

Cholesterol 0 mg

Sodium 869 mg

Carbohydrate 34 g

Dietary Fiber 8 g

Sugars 6 g

Protein 11 g

1. Spread one side of each bread slice with 2 tsp margarine. Place 2 slices bread, margarine-side down, in nonstick skillet coated with cooking spray over medium heat. Top each of these with 2 slices tomato, 1 slice cheese, and 6 slices zucchini. Sprinkle with seasoned salt and pepper. Top with the remaining slices of bread, margarine side up.

2. When the sandwiches are lightly browned on one side, turn them over using a spatula. Continue cooking until lightly browned on second side and cheese is melted. Cut each sandwich in half and serve.

Peppery Cheese Bites

Preparation Time:
10 minutes

Servings: 25

Serving Size:
1 square

This easy appetizer is sure to be a hit!

Cooking spray

2 cups grated Monterey Jack cheese

2 cups fat-free grated cheddar cheese

1 cup pickled banana pepper slices, drained

3 medium eggs

6 egg whites

Paprika

Cost per Serving

1. Preheat oven to 350°F. Coat an 8 × 8-inch baking dish with cooking spray. Combine cheeses and layer half of cheese mixture in bottom of pan. Sprinkle with banana peppers, then remaining cheese.

2. In a mixing bowl, combine eggs and egg whites, beating well. Pour egg mixture evenly over entire pan. Bake for 30 minutes or until set.

3. Remove from oven and sprinkle with paprika. Cool 10 minutes and slice into 25 equal servings. Serve warm. Refrigerate leftovers.

Exchanges

1 Lean Meat

Calories 51

Calories from Fat 27

Total Fat 3 g

Saturated Fat 2 g

Cholesterol 34 mg

Sodium 211 mg

Carbohydrate 1 g

Dietary Fiber 0 g

Sugars 0 g

Protein 5 g

$0.40

Cost per Serving

Creamy Apple-Cinnamon Sandwich Spread

Cottage cheese lends creaminess to this lightly sweet sandwich spread.

2 cups fat-free cottage cheese

3 packets NutraSweet artificial sweetener

1/4 tsp ground cinnamon

1/4 cup finely chopped raisins

1/2 cup finely diced unpeeled red apple

1. Place cottage cheese in a blender or food processor and blend or process until smooth. Pour into medium bowl and stir in sweetener and cinnamon.
2. Gently mix in raisins and apple. Cover and chill for 30 minutes before serving.

Exchanges

1 Carbohydrate

1 Very Lean Meat

Calories 117

Calories from Fat 5

Total Fat <1 g

Saturated Fat <1 g

Cholesterol 0 mg

Sodium 302 mg

Carbohydrate 13 g

Dietary Fiber 1 g

Sugars 8 g

Protein 15 g

Fats, Sweets, and Alcohol

Cost per Serving

Exchanges

1/2 Fat

Calories 20

Calories from Fat
18

Total Fat 2 g

Saturated Fat <1 g

Cholesterol 0 mg

Sodium 50 mg

Carbohydrate <1 g

Dietary Fiber 0 g

Sugars 0 g

Protein 0 g

Herbed Margarine

Lightly flavored with thyme and dill weed, this spread is marvelous on warm, crusty bread or steaming hot baked potatoes.

8 oz reduced-calorie tub margarine, softened

1 tsp dried thyme

1 tsp dried dill weed

1/8 tsp salt

1. Place softened margarine in a mixing bowl and stir in thyme, dill weed, and salt.
2. Store in refrigerator in tightly covered container. The spread is best if refrigerated for at least one hour before serving to allow flavors to blend.

Tangy Dijon Vinaigrette

Preparation Time:
10 minutes

Servings: 6

Serving Size:
2 Tbsp

Drizzle this dressing over a crispy green salad, or use it to marinate fresh, raw vegetables.

1/4 cup canola oil

1/4 cup fat-free, reduced-sodium chicken broth

2 Tbsp white vinegar

1 tsp fresh-squeezed lemon juice

2 Tbsp Dijon mustard

1 green onion, very finely diced

1 tsp minced garlic

1/8 tsp ground black pepper

Cost per Serving

1. Place all ingredients in a small jar, cover tightly with lid, and shake to combine.
2. Refrigerate at least 1 hour to allow flavors to blend. Store leftovers in refrigerator.

Exchanges

2 Fat

Calories 87

Calories from Fat
   81

Total Fat 9 g

Saturated Fat 1 g

Cholesterol 0 mg

Sodium 122 mg

Carbohydrate 1 g

Dietary Fiber <1 g

Sugars <1 g

Protein <1 g

Basic Brown Gravy

Preparation Time:
5 minutes

Servings: 9

Serving Size:
1/4 cup

Cost per Serving

Exchanges

1/2 Starch

1/2 Fat

Calories 59

Calories from Fat
27

Total Fat 3 g

Saturated Fat <1 g

Cholesterol 1 mg

Sodium 65 mg

Carbohydrate 6 g

Dietary Fiber <1 g

Sugars 2 g

Protein 2 g

Serve over biscuits, beef roast, or pork roast.

1 1/2 Tbsp corn oil

1/4 cup all-purpose flour

2 cups fat-free (skim) milk

1/2 cup cold water

1/8 tsp ground black pepper

1/8 tsp salt

2 cubes reduced-sodium beef bouillon dissolved in
    1/4 cup hot water

Kitchen Bouquet, optional

1. Place oil in a large skillet over medium-high heat. Combine flour, milk, 1/2 cup cold water, pepper, and salt in a jar, cover tightly, and shake to mix well. Pour milk mixture into hot oil and cook, stirring constantly with a wire whisk, until it begins to thicken, about 1 or 2 minutes.

2. Add bouillon dissolved in hot water and continue cooking, whisking constantly, until thickened, about 3 minutes. If a darker brown gravy is preferred, add several drops Kitchen Bouquet (usually found in spice aisle) until desired color is achieved.

164

Broiled Pineapple Rings

Preparation Time:
  5 minutes

Servings: 5

Serving Size:
  2 slices

This eye-pleasing dessert is simple and quick.
Serve it hot from the oven.

1 20-oz can sliced pineapple rings in juice, drained
    (1 can should contain 10 rings)

10 maraschino cherries, drained and rinsed

3 Tbsp + 1 tsp light brown sugar

5 tsp reduced-calorie stick margarine, melted

Ground cinnamon

Cost per Serving

1. Preheat broiler. Lay drained pineapple rings in a single layer on a 9 × 13-inch pan with sides—allow edges of pineapple rings to touch.

2. Place a cherry in the center of each pineapple ring. Sprinkle each pineapple ring with 1 tsp brown sugar, then drizzle with 1/2 tsp margarine. Sprinkle with cinnamon.

3. Place 5 inches from broiler and broil (with oven door cracked) for 5 minutes or until topping is bubbly.

Exchanges

2 Carbohydrate

1 Fat

Calories 164

Calories from Fat
  36

Total Fat 4 g

Saturated Fat 1 g

Cholesterol 0 mg

Sodium 91 mg

Carbohydrate 33 g

Dietary Fiber 1 g

Sugars 22 g

Protein <1 g

Cost per Serving

Exchanges

2 Carbohydrate

1 Fat

Calories 197

Calories from Fat
81

Total Fat 9 g

Saturated Fat 3 g

Cholesterol 9 mg

Sodium 168 mg

Carbohydrate 26 g

Dietary Fiber 1 g

Sugars 18 g

Protein 3 g

Cheery Black Cherry Salad

Serve on a lettuce leaf and garnish with lightly toasted coconut if desired.

1 15-oz can pitted dark sweet cherries

1 8-oz package "1/3 less fat" cream cheese, softened

1 tsp vanilla extract

1 8-oz container frozen "lite" whipped topping, thawed

1 8-oz can crushed pineapple in juice, drained

1/4 cup grated coconut

1. Drain juice off cherries and reserve. Slice cherries in half.

2. In a large bowl, whip softened cream cheese with an electric mixer until light and fluffy. Add vanilla extract, 5 Tbsp reserved cherry juice, and whipped topping. Whip until combined.

3. Stir in cherries, drained pineapple, and coconut. Spoon into 8 × 8-inch pan and chill for 2 hours. Cut into 9 equal squares before serving (it will be very soft, so you may prefer to spoon it out).

Creamy Fruit Whip

Preparation Time:
15 minutes

Servings: 10

Serving Size:
1/2 cup

For a special touch, garnish each dish with a whole strawberry or a sprinkle of fresh blueberries.

2 8-oz packages fat-free cream cheese

1 tub sugar-free lemonade mix (enough to make 2 quarts lemonade)

1 8-oz container frozen "lite" whipped topping, thawed

1 cup crushed strawberries (fresh or unsweetened frozen)

Cost per Serving

1. Place cream cheese and lemonade mix in large bowl. Beat with an electric mixer on medium speed until fluffy and smooth. Gently fold in whipped topping, then strawberries, mixing until combined.

2. Pour into individual serving dishes if desired. Cover and refrigerate 2 hours or until of a slightly firmer consistency. Stir twice during chilling.

Exchanges

1 Carbohydrate

1/2 Fat

Calories 103

Calories from Fat 27

Total Fat 3 g

Saturated Fat <1 g

Cholesterol 1 mg

Sodium 395 mg

Carbohydrate 12 g

Dietary Fiber 1 g

Sugars 6 g

Protein 7 g

$0.37

Cost per Serving

Rainbow Parfaits

Here's a refreshing and very simple dessert!

2 cups rainbow sherbet

1 8-oz container sugar-free, fat-free vanilla yogurt

1/4 cup raspberry 100% fruit spread, heated

1. Place 1/2 cup sherbet in each of four parfait glasses.
2. Drizzle each with 2 oz (1/4 container) yogurt then 1 Tbsp heated raspberry spread. Serve immediately.

Exchanges

2 1/2 Carbohydrate

Calories 181

Calories from Fat 5

Total Fat <1 g

Saturated Fat 0 g

Cholesterol 1 mg

Sodium 73 mg

Carbohydrate 41 g

Dietary Fiber <1 g

Sugars 38 g

Protein 3 g

Chocolate Lovers' Frozen Mousse

This creamy chocolate mousse is laced with mini chocolate chips.

2 1.4-oz boxes sugar-free instant chocolate pudding mix

3 cups fat-free (skim) milk

1/4 tsp cinnamon

16 oz frozen "lite" whipped topping, thawed

1/2 cup mini chocolate chips

1. Place pudding mix, milk, and cinnamon in a large mixing bowl. Beat with an electric mixer on medium speed until pudding mix is dissolved.
2. Add whipped topping and mix on low speed until smooth. Gently stir in chocolate chips.
3. Cover tightly and freeze until firm (about 3 hours). To serve, scoop into bowls using an ice cream scoop.

Preparation Time: 10 minutes

Servings: 12

Serving Size: 2 scoops, or 1 cup

$0.32

Cost per Serving

Exchanges

1 1/2 Carbohydrate

1 Fat

Calories 163

Calories from Fat 63

Total Fat 7 g

Saturated Fat <1 g

Cholesterol 3 mg

Sodium 136 mg

Carbohydrate 22 g

Dietary Fiber <1 g

Sugars 14 g

Protein 3 g

Banana-Split Parfaits

Thers parfaits are reminiscent of the old-fashioned favorite banana split.

1 1.4-oz box sugar-free instant chocolate pudding mix

2 cups fat-free (skim) milk

1 banana, sliced

1 8-oz can crushed pineapple in juice, drained

1/4 cup strawberry 100% fruit spread

1/4 cup frozen "lite" whipped topping, thawed

4 maraschino cherries

1. In a mixing bowl, combine pudding and milk, then beat with an electric mixer on low speed until well blended (about 1 to 2 minutes).
2. Layer 1/4 cup pudding in each of 4 parfait glasses. Let stand 5 minutes, then top each with 1/4 of banana slices, 1/4 of pineapple, 1 Tbsp strawberry fruit spread, and another 1/4 cup pudding.
3. Garnish with 1 Tbsp whipped topping and a maraschino cherry. Serve immediately.

Exchanges

3 Carbohydrate

Calories 205

Calories from Fat 9

Total Fat 1 g

Saturated Fat <1 g

Cholesterol 2 mg

Sodium 173 mg

Carbohydrate 43 g

Dietary Fiber 1 g

Sugars 30 g

Protein 6 g

Mocha Freeze

Preparation Time:
15 minutes

Servings: 18

Serving Size:
2 scoops

$0.17

Cost per Serving

Leftovers can be refrozen and beaten smooth again.

4 cups fat-free (skim) milk

2 1/4-oz envelopes unflavored gelatin

6 oz dry sugar-free hot chocolate mix

1 cup cold coffee

2 tsp vanilla extract

1. In a small saucepan, combine 2 cups milk with gelatin and place over medium heat; heat until gelatin is dissolved while stirring constantly.

2. Add hot chocolate mix and continue cooking and stirring until mix is dissolved. Add remaining 2 cups milk, coffee, and vanilla extract; stir well.

3. Pour into a 9 × 13-inch pan and freeze for 3 hours or until firm. Remove from freezer and thaw slightly.

4. Break into chunks with a knife and place in large mixing bowl. Beat with electric mixer on high speed until smooth. Scoop into bowls and serve immediately.

Exchanges
1/2 Carbohydrate

Calories 57
Calories from Fat 5
Total Fat <1 g
Saturated Fat <1 g
Cholesterol 4 mg
Sodium 122 mg
Carbohydrate 8 g
Dietary Fiber <1 g
Sugars 2 g
Protein 5 g

$0.23

Cost per Serving

Exchanges

1 1/2 Carbohydrate

Calories 122

Calories from Fat
18

Total Fat 2 g

Saturated Fat <1 g

Cholesterol 48 mg

Sodium 102 mg

Carbohydrate 21 g

Dietary Fiber <1 g

Sugars 3 g

Protein 5 g

Creamy Pumpkin Custard

Allspice, with its mingling of the tastes of cloves, nutmeg, and cinnamon, can often be substituted for cloves and/or nutmeg in recipes. It is a marvelous spice to keep on hand!

Cooking spray

3 2-inch graham cracker squares, finely crushed

1 15-oz can pumpkin

1 12-oz can evaporated skim milk

1/4 cup packed dark brown sugar

1/4 tsp brown sugar substitute

1 whole egg + 2 egg whites

1 tsp cinnamon

1/4 tsp allspice

1 tsp vanilla extract

1/2 cup + 1 Tbsp fat-free whipped topping

1. Preheat oven to 325°F. Coat an 8 × 8-inch baking dish with cooking spray. Sprinkle graham cracker crumbs evenly across bottom of pan.

2. In a large mixing bowl, combine pumpkin, milk, sweeteners, eggs, cinnamon, allspice, and vanilla extract. Mix well using an electric mixer on medium speed.

3. Pour custard into baking dish and bake for 50 minutes to 1 hour or until a knife inserted into the center comes out clean.

4. Place pan on cooling rack and cool for 20 minutes. Cut into 9 equal servings and top each with 1 Tbsp whipped topping. May chill if desired. Refrigerate leftovers.

No-Bake Peanut Butter Treats

Here's a simple dessert or snack that uses staple items from the kitchen pantry.

1/2 cup reduced-fat creamy peanut butter

2 Tbsp unsweetened apple juice

1 tsp vanilla extract

1/8 tsp ground cinnamon

1/2 cup raisins

4 2-inch graham cracker squares, crushed

1/2 cup cornflake cereal

1 Tbsp powdered sugar

1. In a large mixing bowl, cream together peanut butter, apple juice, vanilla extract, and cinnamon. Stir in raisins, graham crackers, and cereal.

2. Roll mixture into 1 1/2-inch balls and place on baking sheet. Refrigerate 1 hour, then roll each ball in powdered sugar to coat. Store in tightly covered cookie tin in refrigerator—will maintain freshness for 3 to 4 days.

$0.14

Cost per Serving

Exchanges

1 Carbohydrate

1 Fat

Calories 121

Calories from Fat 45

Total Fat 5 g

Saturated Fat 1 g

Cholesterol 0 mg

Sodium 112 mg

Carbohydrate 15 g

Dietary Fiber 1 g

Sugars 6 g

Protein 4 g

Peach Cobble-Up

$0.13

Cost per Serving

Serve warm with a steaming cup of coffee or tea!

1 cup biscuit mix

1/4 cup packed dark brown sugar

1/2 tsp ground nutmeg

1 tsp ground cinnamon

1 Tbsp reduced-calorie stick margarine, softened

1/3 cup fat-free (skim) milk

Cooking spray

1 16-oz can sliced peaches in juice, drain and
    reserve juice

1. Preheat oven to 400°F. In a large mixing bowl, combine biscuit mix, brown sugar, nutmeg, and cinnamon. Using an electric mixer on low, mix in softened margarine until mixture is crumbly. Add milk and blend thoroughly.

2. Spread batter evenly on bottom of an 8-inch square pan coated with cooking spray. Place peach slices on top of batter. Pour reserved juice evenly over peaches.

3. Bake for 30 minutes. Slice into 9 equal squares. Refrigerate leftovers then reheat before serving.

Exchanges

1 1/2 Carbohydrate

Calories 99

Calories from Fat 9

Total Fat 1 g

Saturated Fat <1 g

Cholesterol <1 mg

Sodium 151 mg

Carbohydrate 22 g

Dietary Fiber 1 g

Sugars 6 g

Protein 2 g

Blackberry Dumplings

Preparation Time:
 10 minutes

Servings: 6

Serving Size:
 1 cup

Here's a stovetop version of old-fashioned blackberry pie. Pick your own berries for significant savings!

$0.77

Cost per Serving

4 cups fresh or 2 bags (16 oz each) unsweetened frozen blackberries, thawed

15 packets saccharin artificial sweetener

1/4 cup sugar

3 cups water

1 Tbsp reduced-calorie stick margarine

Dumplings

1 2/3 cups all-purpose flour

2 tsp baking powder

2 Tbsp sugar

1/8 tsp salt

1 cup fat-free (skim) milk

1. Place berries, sweetener, sugar, water, and margarine in large, widemouthed pan. Bring to a boil; cover and simmer 10 minutes over low heat.
2. Meanwhile in a large bowl, combine flour, baking powder, sugar, and salt. Add milk and mix to form a soft dough.
3. Drop dough by tablespoons onto blackberries. Increase heat to medium-high and bring berries to a boil.
4. Reduce heat to low, cover pan with lid, and simmer 35 minutes. Serve warm. Refrigerate leftovers. When reheating leftovers, thin with water as desired.

Exchanges

3 1/2 Carbohydrate

Calories 266

Calories from Fat 18

Total Fat 2 g

Saturated Fat <1 g

Cholesterol 1 mg

Sodium 257 mg

Carbohydrate 56 g

Dietary Fiber 5 g

Sugars 20 g

Protein 6 g

Cost per Serving

Classic Apple Crisp

If you have apples that have lost their crispness, don't throw them away—use them in this cobbler!

3 cups thinly sliced, peeled apple

Cooking spray

1 Tbsp lemon juice

1/2 tsp ground cinnamon

1/4 cup sugar

Topping

1/4 cup all-purpose flour

1/2 cup brown sugar

2 Tbsp reduced-calorie stick margarine

1/4 cup quick-cooking oats

1. Preheat oven to 375°F. Place apples in an 8-inch square baking dish coated with cooking spray. Sprinkle with lemon juice, cinnamon, and sugar. Cover with foil and bake for 45 minutes.

2. In a mixing bowl, combine flour, brown sugar, and margarine using a pastry blender and mixing until crumbly. Stir in oats.

3. Remove foil from cooked fruit and top with oatmeal mixture. Bake uncovered for 20 minutes or until topping is golden.

Exchanges

3 Carbohydrate

Calories 194

Calories from Fat 18

Total Fat 2 g

Saturated Fat <1 g

Cholesterol 0 mg

Sodium 54 mg

Carbohydrate 43 g

Dietary Fiber 2 g

Sugars 18 g

Protein 1 g

Simple Strawberry Shortcake

Warmed strawberry fruit spread serves as a quick topping for these simple shortcakes.

Shortcakes

2 1/3 cups biscuit mix

2 Tbsp sugar

3 Tbsp reduced-calorie stick margarine, melted

1/2 cup fat-free (skim) milk

1/2 tsp vanilla extract

Topping

1 1/4 cups strawberry 100% fruit spread, heated

1/2 cup frozen "lite" whipped topping, thawed

1. Preheat oven to 425°F. Combine biscuit mix, sugar, margarine, milk, and extract in a large mixing bowl. Stir until ingredients are combined and a soft dough forms—dough will be sticky.
2. Turn dough out onto waxed paper dusted with flour and knead 10 times with floured hands. Using a floured rolling pin, roll dough to 1/2-inch thickness, and cut into 10 cakes with a 2 1/2-inch floured round cookie or biscuit cutter.
3. Place dough on ungreased baking sheet and bake at 425°F for 10–14 minutes or until light golden.
4. Split each shortcake in half. Drizzle each bottom with 1 Tbsp heated fruit spread, then top with 1 Tbsp whipped topping. Replace shortcake tops and drizzle each with 1 Tbsp heated fruit spread. Serve immediately.

Preparation Time: 15 minutes

Servings: 10

Serving Size: 1 shortcake

$0.30

Cost per Serving

Exchanges

1 1/2 Carbohydrate

Calories 114

Calories from Fat 18

Total Fat 2 g

Saturated Fat <1 g

Cholesterol 1 mg

Sodium 278 mg

Carbohydrate 22 g

Dietary Fiber <1 g

Sugars 22 g

Protein 2 g

$0.13

Cost per Serving

Individual Cinnamon Crumb Cakes

Serve for dessert or at a weekend brunch.

1/2 cup all-purpose flour
1/2 cup sugar
1 dash salt
1 tsp baking powder
1/2 cup fat-free (skim) milk
1 tsp vanilla extract
3 Tbsp reduced-calorie stick margarine, melted
Cooking spray

Topping
2 Tbsp all-purpose flour
1/4 cup packed brown sugar
1 Tbsp reduced-calorie stick margarine
1/2 tsp ground cinnamon

Exchanges

4 Carbohydrate

Calories 290

Calories from Fat
54

Total Fat 6 g

Saturated Fat 1 g

Cholesterol 1 mg

Sodium 274 mg

Carbohydrate 56 g

Dietary Fiber 1 g

Sugars 26 g

Protein 3 g

1. Preheat oven to 375°F. In a large mixing bowl, combine flour, sugar, salt, and baking powder. Add milk, vanilla extract, and melted margarine, stirring just until dry ingredients are moistened.

2. Spoon batter into 4 6-oz custard cups coated with cooking spray. Place custard cups on baking sheet before putting in oven. Bake cakes for 20 minutes.

3. Meanwhile, combine flour, brown sugar, margarine, and cinnamon, then mix with a pastry cutter or fork until crumbly—set aside.

4. After cakes have baked for 20 minutes, open oven and sprinkle cakes evenly with crumb topping (do not remove cakes from oven). Bake an additional 5 minutes or until cooked through. Serve in custard cups while still warm.

Vanilla Custard Sauce

Preparation Time:
10 minutes

Servings: 7

Serving Size:
1/3 cup

Cost per Serving

Drizzle over fresh fruit, angel food cake, or leftover muffins that are split in half.

2 cups fat-free (skim) milk

2 Tbsp cornstarch

1/2 cup liquid egg substitute

2 Tbsp reduced-calorie stick margarine

1 1/2 tsp vanilla extract

10 packets NutraSweet artificial sweetener

1. In a large saucepan, combine milk, cornstarch, and egg substitute. Whisk until well mixed. Add margarine, then place pan over medium heat. Cook uncovered about 8 minutes or until custard thickens.
2. Once custard begins to heat and thicken, whisk constantly to prevent sticking. Remove from heat and whisk in vanilla extract and sweetener. Serve warm.
3. Refrigerate leftovers—will thicken upon chilling. May be eaten cold as a custard rather than as a sauce.

Exchanges

1/2 Carbohydrate

1/2 Fat

Calories 66

Calories from Fat
18

Total Fat 2 g

Saturated Fat <1 g

Cholesterol 1 mg

Sodium 105 mg

Carbohydrate 7 g

Dietary Fiber <1 g

Sugars 3 g

Protein 5 g

Banana-Cream Fruit Dip

Servings: 8

Serving Size:
1/4 cup

$0.25

Cost per Serving

Try this simple dip for fresh fruit.

1 0.9-oz package sugar-free, fat-free instant banana-cream pudding mix

3/4 cup fat-free (skim) milk

1 8-oz can crushed pineapple in juice, drain and reserve juice

1/2 cup fat-free sour cream

1. In a large bowl, combine pudding mix, milk, and reserved pineapple juice. Mix with an electric mixer until smooth (will be thick). Add sour cream and mix again until smooth.

2. Stir in pineapple and chill for 30 minutes.

Exchanges

1/2 Carbohydrate

Calories 53

Calories from Fat 5

Total Fat <1 g

Saturated Fat <1 g

Cholesterol <1 mg

Sodium 180 mg

Carbohydrate 9 g

Dietary Fiber <1 g

Sugars 5 g

Protein 3 g

Chocolate-Banana Shake

Preparation Time:
5 minutes

Servings: 1

Serving Size:
1 shake

This frosty recipe for one can be doubled to serve a friend too!

1/4 cup fat-free (skim) milk

1 cup sugar-free vanilla ice cream

1 Tbsp sugar-free instant chocolate milk mix

1/4 ripe banana

1. Place all ingredients in blender and blend until thick and smooth.

$0.48

Cost per Serving

Exchanges

2 1/2 Carbohydrate

2 Fat

Calories 273

Calories from Fat
81

Total Fat 9 g

Saturated Fat <1 g

Cholesterol 31 mg

Sodium 175 mg

Carbohydrate 39 g

Dietary Fiber 2 g

Sugars 7 g

Protein 9 g

Wild Berry Syrup

Preparation Time:
15 minutes

Servings: 10

Serving Size:
1/4 cup

$0.15

Cost per Serving

This syrup is delicious over Cinnamon French Toast, p. 81, pancakes, waffles, or sugar-free ice cream.

1 cup water

1 0.3-oz package sugar-free wild berry–flavored gelatin

1 12-oz package fresh blueberries or unsweetened frozen blueberries, thawed

1/2 cup cold water

1 1/2 Tbsp cornstarch

1. In a large saucepan, bring 1 cup water to a boil. Add gelatin and whisk until dissolved. Stir in blueberries, reduce heat to medium, bring to a simmer, and cook uncovered for 5 minutes.

2. In a liquid measuring cup, combine cold water and cornstarch, stirring until cornstarch is dissolved. Add cornstarch mixture to berry mixture, increase heat to high, bring to a boil, and cook 1 minute, whisking constantly.

3. Place 1 cup of mixture in blender, cover, and process until smooth. Pour fruit puree into a serving container, then stir in remaining blueberry mixture. Serve warm. Refrigerate leftovers—will gel with cooling. Rewarm over low heat when it's time to serve again.

Exchanges

1/2 Fruit

Calories 29

Calories from Fat 5

Total Fat <1 g

Saturated Fat 0 g

Cholesterol 0 mg

Sodium 26 mg

Carbohydrate 5 g

Dietary Fiber 2 g

Sugars 2 g

Protein 1 g

Index

ALPHABETICAL LIST OF RECIPES

SUBJECT INDEX